IT'S NOT MY FAULT

Reclaiming Leadership and Values

ROSE CATALANO

It's Not My Fault
Copyright © 2021 by Rose Catalano

ISBN
978-1-956529-39-5 (Paperback)
978-1-956529-40-1 (eBook)

"Everything flows, and Nothing abides,
Everything gives way, and
Nothing stays fixed."

—Heraclitus

This book is dedicated to my daughter, Sabina, and my son, David, whose search for authenticity not only matches but surpasses my own.

May every hour of every day be filled with wonder.

Love, mom/rc

IT'S NOT MY FAULT

"Knowledge is of no value unless you put it into practice."

— *Anton Pavlovich Chekhov*

TABLE OF CONTENTS

PROLOGUE

Do you often find yourself so busy that you can't even afford to take a short break? Are you too busy to set priorities? Is your mind so filled with work that you find it hard to relax at the end of the day?

If so, you are not alone. As an independent business owner, I have witnessed enough hustle and bustle over the years to make anyone's head spin. I've heard stories from other business people that could serve as the plot lines for movies and TV shows. I've had that frustrating but all-too-common experience of seeing an entire day disappear in what feels like a few minutes, only to realize that the pile of work on my desk hasn't budged an inch.

For over three decades, I've busied myself with the running of two security companies, and as the hands-on owner/operator of these businesses, I have gained substantial experience navigating high-pressure situations. Almost every day on the job brought new stresses and challenges. I've met make-or-break project deadlines that threatened serious consequences if I was a minute late. I've learned to keep my composure when an odd tingling sensation took hold of my nerves as I faced agendas that seemed impossible to work through. I have sweated through tricky encounters with over-excited employees and confrontational customers. In the end, it all got done because I was able to adopt what I call *"conflict-resolution sensibility."* This mindset, which involves equal doses of grit and diplomacy, rests on the idea that strong values and well-developed people skills can get you through any problem you are likely to face in business or life. This book will show you how to cultivate a conflict-resolution sensibility and apply that mindset to every aspect of your life and career.

Resolving conflict is not always about compromise. It also involves learning how and when to stand your ground, ideally without alienating others. Over the years, I've learned to rely on proven negotiating techniques as a means to pacify uncooperative suppliers and closed-minded officials. There were times when the burdens placed on my business by government regulations became so overwhelming that I considered abandoning entrepreneurship altogether. But I did not give in to the pressure, or give up on my companies. Instead, I stood firm and fought.

Quitting might have been an easy way out, but it wasn't a sensible option for me. The better alternative was to follow my sixth sense and to mitigate those challenging circumstances with optimism and determination. Looking back, I'm glad I didn't let negative experiences or power-plays by rivals and people in authority prevent me from achieving my goals.

In our busy and competitive world, every decision we make, whether at work or at home, serves as a reflection of our beliefs, values, hopes, and ambitions. Our beliefs and actions amount to a collective set of statements about what we value most in life, and how we plan to pursue and achieve our dreams. Every creative idea has the potential to become a reality. Every minute of every day, our actions both reflect and determine how we have chosen to live, and how we plan to move forward with our life.

I often encounter people who feel overwhelmed or discouraged by the hand they've been dealt. They weren't born rich, or they didn't get enough emotional support growing up, or they lack self-esteem, or doubt their ability to compete in today's business world. I remind them of the old Roman proverb, *"Carpe Diem,"* which, as most of us know by now, means to "seize the day." *Carpe Diem* reminds us of the simple truth that we all have agency — or the power to change our own lives — and that we can and must chase our own happiness. Seizing the day means not passing up an opportunity to further your career or to improve some other aspect of your life. It can mean taking the opportunity to treat yourself to something you've longed for.

Seizing the day means not letting hesitation or fear hold you back.

To live according to the values set out by this well-known Latin phrase, you may need to evolve. The first and most important step involves finding the self-discipline to overcome fear.

Whenever you feel hesitant about something you know, deep down, could improve your life or your business, force yourself to take the opportunity or do the thing that's scaring you. Connect with the fear, recognize it for what it so often is — an opportunity to grow — and take the step that your cautious mind is telling you to avoid.

Of course, there are real dangers in the world, and I'm not suggesting you embrace those. But if you're faced with an opportunity and you're scared because you'll have to extend yourself beyond your comfort zone, that's your cue to advance, not retreat. Make the switch from hesitation to facilitation and avoid falling into the trap of guessing how things might have been if only a lack of courage and self-confidence had not sabotaged the opportunity. By taking action, you will inevitably learn something you need to know. This works in your favour, whether the initial risk proves fruitful or not. It is by taking action and pushing through discomfort that we grow. When this happens, we get smarter. The smarter we become, the closer we get to achieving our potential and realizing our dreams.

Decades of experience with this cycle of pushing through uncertainty, seizing opportunity, and achieving my goals has left me with a burning desire to share my insights into this process. As I thought about the everyday practices and values that most resonated with me, I was driven to grab a pen and paper and jot down the full list.

But the list that keeps evolving and harmonizing in my head is too long. I've had to settle for an abbreviated version that highlights only the most important qualities I believe make us who we are and what we stand for. These are:

LOVE

Although we associate love with making the heart skip a beat, love is also that special emotion that brings a natural feeling of sharing and personal contentment. In the grand scheme of things, without love, material possessions mean little. Loving what we do, loving others, and loving to help people in need, all work to generate a feedback loop of positivity. The more love we give and receive, the happier and less anxious we are. When we have the support of someone we love, we're better equipped to face and cope with daily stressors.

CREATIVITY

Being creative engages the mind and allows us to shake off obstacles. Creativity encourages us to seek out ways to lift our spirits — by reading, shopping, cooking, talking to a friend, going for long walks, or listening to music, for example. Creativity allows us to try new strategies for solving problems, and can boost morale when we're feeling down or discouraged. When we're creative, we challenge old habits and routines and figure out new ways to make our life and work more fun.

EFFECTIVENESS

To be effective is to put in motion the capabilities that produce desired results. Being effective connects us to our intentions and gets us closer to our goals. To maintain effectiveness one needs to constantly work on practices, know when to take breaks, and be willing to keep learning and developing new skills, long after we leave school. In business, effectiveness equals a healthy bottom line and high-quality results.

FREEDOM

Freedom allows us to be who we are. It gives us the opportunity to voice our opinions and pursue happiness without fear of rejection, restriction, or retribution. Freedom can take many forms. It can be interpreted as individual freedom, political freedom, financial freedom,

freedom of expression, or it can take other forms. Without some or all of these forms of freedom, we can't be our authentic selves, and we can't achieve success in business or life.

Freedom is the bedrock and the minimum requirement for achieving our goals.

LOYALTY

Loyalty is an indispensable quality in relationships and in business. Loyalty implies that a person is serious about keeping commitments and dedications. To be loyal does not mean to be submissive. In business, loyalty translates into enhanced productivity, reduced turnover, and improved margins.

INTEGRITY

This is a core quality for leadership roles. It demands truthfulness, honesty, and a moral conviction to do what's right. Without integrity, we'll set ourselves up to fail both at work and at home.

DISCIPLINE

Discipline promotes stability and structure, and allows us to be effective in business and in other parts of life. Without some form of discipline, everything and everyone around us would be in a constant state of chaos.

PERSONAL GROWTH

Personal growth refers to the process that helps us develop the capabilities and potential to reach our dreams and aspirations. Growth happens when we push through discomfort and challenge ourselves to learn and do new things.

SIMPLICITY

Living simply does not mean having to make do with less in life. Simplicity helps us focus on what is important, and highlights what is essential to live well. Simplicity also saves energy by cutting out unnecessary processes.

I believe that if you can manage to combine all or most of these traits, qualities, and approaches, you can achieve just about anything you set out to achieve.

Achieving your goals — setting yourself up for success and emotional contentment— requires hard work, perseverance, and solid commitments. It's up to you to figure out how much effort you're willing to put into becoming a productive member of society, and how willing you are to learn from your mistakes.

LEADERS, FOLLOWERS, AND SLACKERS

This book is about identifying and understanding the options available to us both in our everyday life and in the workplace.

We can choose to be a leader, a follower, or a slacker. We might as well make the choice consciously, with an understanding of the costs and benefits of each position.

To be a leader does not mean that one has to have a big title, exceed a certain pay rate, or constantly flaunt one's authority. Leadership means having the determination and drive to motivate others and be in constant pursuit of the greater good.

We may choose to be a follower because it's easier than the alternative. It's certainly easier to be an employee than it is to start a business, be the boss, or even serve as a manager of a group or organization. And it's not always bad to be a follower. This is especially true for anyone who doesn't adjust well to change and who wishes to live their life within their comfort zone.

Choosing to be a slacker is different. A slacker does the least amount possible, often not only in work but also in other parts of life. We can choose to be the person with the least output possible, day in and day out, but we should know the costs of such a decision. We should also know why we're making that choice. Often it's not because of limited options, but because a person is in denial about their situation or simply doesn't see the point of pushing the needle of responsibility too far.

Whatever we choose to do in life, we need to be prepared to take responsibility for our actions or inactions. Only then we can make our way to personal and professional preparedness.

This book explores these three different approaches to life and work. It does so through a combination of anecdotal evidence (stories based on composites of people I have known or heard about, not actual individuals) and my own analysis, drawn in part from philosophy, cognitive science, and books about business. My intention here is to guide the reader through some examples of different approaches you can take to responsibility in life and on the job, and in doing so, to help each person see themselves and their choices more clearly.

ETHICS

Underlying all of this is an argument about ethics. This book starts from the position that personal and business ethics are worth cultivating and preserving. An awareness of ethical practices can set us on the right path for ourselves, our colleagues, our friends, our family members and our employees. Most of us want to live a wonderful life full of riches and good health, but not all of us know how to get there, or are willing to put in the work required to set up strong, ethical relationships in business and life. An understanding of ethics, and a willingness to do the work of putting ethical goals into practice, will take you a very long way. This book aims to show you how to get there.

Unavoidably, some of the examples in this book fall into the category of cautionary tales. While there is great value in highlighting positive examples of ethical behaviour, there is also much to be gained by exploring the consequences of *unethical* behaviour, along with corresponding "lessons learned."

Some of what I have to say here may strike certain readers as too critical. To those readers, I would say: Gentle advice doesn't always get results. If we really want to strengthen our values and live more ethically, sometimes we have to start by gaining a clearer understanding of what we have been saying and doing to harm or diminish ourselves and others up to the point when we decided to make a change.

Part of the impetus for this book comes from my frustration and astonishment with people who consistently underperform in the workplace, and then refuse to take responsibility for their actions. To the extent that my writing explores the problem of dodging responsibility, the whole narrative can be considered an extended cautionary tale.

If you want to leave your values unexamined, and if you're determined to avoid taking full responsibility for the job you do, then you may accomplish a little, but you're unlikely to accomplish a lot. The life of a person who refuses to work hard or take responsibility for their actions is always going to be somewhat stunted. But if you have read this far, then congratulations! That fact alone means that you're truly interested in taking charge of your life, clarifying your value system, and learning to live and work more ethically. In these pages, we'll journey through the good, the bad, and the ugly of workplace values and ethics. By the end, I promise you will have a clearer sense of how to conduct yourself in this complex world of ours. And if you're a business leader, I hope you'll gain a better understanding of why your employees sometimes say and do the things they do, and what can be done to encourage everyone in your organization to take more responsibility for their actions on behalf of the company.

CHAPTER 1

CHAPTER 1

VIEWPOINTS

People like to complain. They like to be heard, and they don't always care if their arguments or opinions are factual or fair.

During my career in the service industry, I have learned to take statements of discontent and claims of wrongfulness seriously, but not *too* seriously. I've heard countless complaints throughout my business days, and many of those have been debatable. Often, when someone complains bitterly to a service provider, they are venting frustrations that began somewhere else. Maybe they fought with their spouse over breakfast. Maybe their teenager told them they hated them. When doing business, and especially when providing a service to the public, it's important to remember that not every statement of discontent is either factual or an invitation to an open-minded discourse. Only by keeping complaints in perspective can we learn how to float through confrontations and not take every attack too much to heart.

Complaints by employees can be similarly suspect. Often, they are based on unsubstantiated claims and are accompanied by weak excuses from employees who lack a viable or valid work philosophy. I have seen verbal and written complaints that are no more than reports of convenience, put forth to benefit someone's unclear point of view. And such complaints rarely turn out well for the employee. Could it be that the habit of constantly complaining and offering excuses is the main reason why things often turnout badly for the people involved?

Complaints and excuses have a way of backfiring, even while they are being uttered. One day, after listening to some employees' bizarre stories in the workplace, I began to write down what I thought were the strangest things people freely go on about at any given moment. Before analyzing those statements, I wondered where they were coming from. Were they saying these outlandish things just to make themselves sound eloquent or 'in the know'? Did they believe they could easily manipulate the other party? Even though it pained me to listen to these incredible tales, I continued recording a host of different dealings and the pages filled up fast. I wrote solely for my sense of bewilderment and without a plan for what to do with the material. Once I began, I found that I could hardly keep up with all of the shady words and frail excuses that came out of people's mouths.

Over time, I became increasingly aware that a lot of people like to talk nonsense, rarely say what they mean, and use fifteen words when they could use five. Once I caught on to this tendency, I saw it everywhere. When that happened, it became very trying not to draw people's attention to their verbal habits. However, keeping my composure in a business setting was more valuable to me than saying what I really wanted to say, and above all, I didn't want to risk creating an awkward situation. Those are the days when I give my moral compass a big thumbs up. Without it, it would be hard to develop the sense of goodness required to be guided in the right direction, and as a result, to have fewer regrets about our behavior.

One day, as my son David and I were discussing a business matter, the subject of the peculiar encounters I had recorded in my notebook came to light. Without a moment's hesitation, he suggested I write a book about them. He felt that some people might find the content amusing, meaningful, hilarious or sad, while others might pick up such a book as an escape from a heavy day's reality.

That suggestion made me think about the value of sharing my experiences and what it might mean to someone else. Because words have the ability to touch people, there was a good chance that talking about my experiences might help someone find their right to be heard. At the same time, I would be clarifying what's most important to me. Telling my story would probably facilitate other people's decision-making process.

In a world where some companies and individuals soar above others by doing things a little differently, it stands to reason that whatever one can learn from other people's experiences could be useful in addressing situations in one's own life and business. Creating a story structure out of the random events that I observed in and outside of my organization might provide useful tips for a curious reader or a progressive entrepreneur. But then, how could I be sure that after I take the time to render these events in a decipherable format, my anecdotes would touch people or perhaps even provide a laugh or two? I worried about my ability to tell the stories the way they needed to be told. But I was not about to drop this project before it started. My motto is: when in doubt, weigh your options, and don't let self- doubt hold you back from seizing an opportunity.

Running the show

To launch a new business or to manage a pre-existing establishment, one must create and adhere to constant operation manual updates. This is true whether the entity is a proprietorship, a partnership, or a corporation. Although the process of keeping operation manuals up to date and ensuring that employees follow them is extremely taxing, it is also rewarding, in that it helps to offset conflicts and prevent misunderstandings, while minimizing operational and financial problems.

Typically, the business path is not a smooth or a straight one, so it comes as no surprise that in the present day, the commercial and industrial landscape is also changing at a rapid pace. One side-effect of all of this frenetic activity and constant change is that principals and upper management rarely have a chance to unplug. Doing business in today's high-speed environment demands constant learning.

However, the fresh and new perspectives that come with the territory do not always bolster production or resilience, or guarantee the ability to take the company to the next level. The need for constant learning makes the entrepreneurial road rather curvy and unpredictable. Maybe that is why we have the old saying, "If it was easy, anybody could do it." As a business owner, I know that the day-to-day battles are real, and that it's all too easy for disagreements to boil over into conflict. However, most of us sign up for this joyride with optimism and good spirit, and we gladly continue to work at it until we can't do it anymore.

One way to succeed in business is by sharing knowledge with others in your field. B2B (business-to-business) sharing of operational wisdom can be an integral part of the overall way products, systems, and services are bundled together to address customers' needs. Learning from others can help business owners and directors avoid mistakes and adopt winning strategies. In business, relying on luck alone does not take us very far, if it moves us at all. We have to work hard and fight hearty battles, and when a little luck romances our efforts, we may see positive results.

By nature, most people have a tendency to conform. Smoothing over conflict keeps us comfortable. But when personal opinions differ or clash with business values, the outcome can put a strain on the corporation's culture and mores. Research suggests that the decision-makers who cannot loosen the reins of their pre-established norms and values are very apt to disregard input from people who hold conflicting opinions. I think our ability to reason things out shows up best when we put on an obliging face — especially in a social setting. In most circumstances, however, we're not always open to accepting divergent suggestions or clearly explaining why we cannot support a position other than our own. This is especially true in the case of an employer-to-employee exchange whereby each one pretends to accept a belief they don't agree with. If both sides are faking it, communication is bound to fail.

Public opinion usually favours employees over employers. Although being on the side of the 'poor employee' may be a justifiable position, sometimes it's just a case of bias. Most of us are inclined to root for the underdog as soon as we hear of an unhappy story. I don't always identify with how and why we react to the blips of our life's radar the way we do, but it may have something to do with our inherent method of response. That being so, then reacting to a gloomy situation that touched a friend, a co-worker, a family member, or even a character that plays the victim in a movie must represent an automated internal response to our outer reality. We all face adversity along the way, and it's how we react to the challenges that define us. I'm a firm believer that every hardship presents us with an opportunity for betterment and a chance to become more resilient.

Being the perceived Goliath in any situation, corporations don't always get a lot of sympathy from the public. When a corporation faces adversity, people tend to think they deserve it or that they have all the resources they need to get out of trouble. We don't often see a corporation as the dark horse in any given situation. It's far more common to hear of people downplaying the hardships that corporations face. But while business owners tend to be out of favour, their problems and challenges are no less real than they are for employees or customers. Everything that goes on in an organization is important to an entrepreneur, and as they get pulled in multiple directions all at once, they must not lose sight of their moral codes, or let anyone drag them down. When the unbearable happens and they get knocked down, it may take a little while, but most of them will get back up.

For a business owner, to fail is to learn. Most of the people who manage to launch a business enterprise are focused on getting results, and are not easily deterred by setbacks. But it might come as a surprise to learn that many business owners also suffer from intense worry and even a lack of confidence, at least at some stages of their career. The pain of having to put out fires (albeit, we hope, figurative ones) at any given time of day or night is real, and may actually take some employees aback once they allow themselves to be awoken from their dream of separation. Perhaps, once they step away from their pre-determined frame of mind, employees will dig deeper and acknowledge that their employer is just a person, with a vision, who is willing to go through the ringer to make that vision a reality. It can be hard for employees to see this when they are caught up in viewing their employer as an adversary. Such people practice selective empathy, and would rather side with the majority than respond to the reality in front of them. It might be for that reason that business owners are notorious for pretending that everything is fine and projecting an image of themselves as cool, collected, and successful.

In light of all of this, my son's suggestion that I turn my stray notes and observations into a book began to seem like an excellent idea. He seemed to detect the importance of story-sharing in the service industry right from the onset. The plan to keep my annotations hidden in a drawer must have caused a cramp in his stomach every time he thought about it. He probably worried that by leaving my notes on workplace confrontations and other testy events dormant; I was giving a free pass to individuals who cause chaos in the workplace. If everyone were to give them a pass, just because it's easier than the alternative, how will they ever learn to be more positive and productive? Who or what will set them on a better path, and discourage them from interfering with important dealings in the workplace? Likewise, if curtailing the poor performance of some employees is impossible, then maybe we can at least convince them to slow down and exercise more caution. Employees need to understand how their day-to-day actions and interactions affect the bottom line of the businesses that employ them. Rude or inconsiderate behaviour and careless actions can cause profits to vanish. My collected stories demonstrate exactly how this happens, and what can be done about it. I would let my cohorts, counterparts and competitors know they were not the sole players in this game and remind them that somehow, in the end, strategic thinking usually prevails. Even if we don't have all the correct answers, by applying a razor-edged tool called *strategy*, we can mitigate uncertainty, leverage opportunity, and smooth over rough patches.

Of course, not many people are inclined to support and cheer for the entrepreneur, and nothing will change if our stories are not shared and we don't outline the key takeaways from each story so we can all learn from it.

When I began to work on this book, I had no preconceived plan, no outline, and no theme in place. As the author of three other books, I know how much time and energy it takes to bring an idea from its roughest initial form to its finished state, in the shape of a book that people can hold in their hands. I've faced all of this with my other three book projects. *This Head of Security Wears High Heels* was the training ground and the beginning of my writing experience. That book was my way of telling the story of how I saw some old traditions serve as obstacles that hampered female academic and social advancement. In it, I argued that the ability to succeed in any given field should not be determined by gender but by one's ability to set and achieve goals. *A Child's Voyage to New Life* was the project that almost put a squeeze on my brain as I tried to think through my experiences of growing up in a sexist society. I thought about all of the times I witnessed young girls being shoved aside because their voices were not strong enough to push through the barriers erected by powerful men. Moreover, that book showed how, through sheer determination and willpower, I was able to turn a trying situation into a positive outcome. *Emotions of Retirement* grew out of my desire to explain how I imagined exiting the workplace that I've called my second home for so long. While telling that story, I also wanted to bring to light the importance of having a strategic financial plan in place in order to make the retirement years an enjoyable time.

This Head of Security Wears High Heels

Rose Catalano

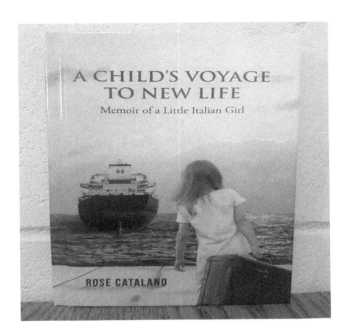

A CHILD'S VOYAGE TO NEW LIFE

Memoir of a Little Italian Girl

ROSE CATALANO

In life, it's important to read, and for some of us, it's equally important to write. This can be true for a multitude of reasons. Some of us write in order to share our ideas with the world, or to affirm our own narratives. Some of us read and write to broaden our vocabulary, our world view, or our ability to communicate.

Words! More words! Spoken words! Written words! Do words really matter? Yes, as a matter of fact, I'm of the opinion that they do. Yet it's obvious to me that not everyone holds to this sacred truth. The people whose words I've collected here often seem to believe that they can say anything, fail to follow through, and never face any consequences. The tone and body language in which some of the words are spoken has always given me the impression that a good number of people have mastered the art of evasion. They don't even believe they should make apologies to anyone as they mete out their verbal tricks.

As my notes file grew, I began to hear conversations from earlier in the day as though they were favourite songs set for continuous replay. Eventually, I traced it back to its source: my son's suggestion to write a book based on my stories collected from the workplace and other areas of life. Writing about real life events and talking about some of the signals within that realm could have emotional resonance for many people and could even generate awareness of the realities that entrepreneurs face every day. It may be hard to believe, but writing about true events and practical strategies can sometimes be as hard as writing invented stories. Non- fiction is a form of creation, and it takes skill to convert the events of our lives into a readable narrative. As Mark Twain once said

"Truth is stranger than fiction, but it is because Fiction is obliged to stick to possibilities; Truth ain't."

The thing that finally convinced me to write this book was a minor but baffling exchange involving an employee and a scheduling manager. The employee had sent an email to the manager in the wee hours of the morning, and inside that email was a bizarre request. "I want you to give me lots of hours of work in the coming weeks," it stated, "but, I cannot guarantee that I'll show up to the assigned shifts." The scheduling officer stared at the email in astonishment. And really, what was a busy manager to make of such a request? As any reasonable person knows, it makes no sense to ask for "lots of hours of work" while in the same breath acknowledging that you may not show up for the shifts that you are assigned. Clearly, this employee had come to us from the College of Unsolvable Riddles and Oxymorons. The more I thought about this exchange, the more convinced I became of the need for a book that would dissect examples of workplace communication like this one, carefully separate the sources and modes of irrationality brought on by such exchanges, and offer some better ways for employees to speak to each other, and to their supervisors, in the workplace.

Taking a quick glance at the scribbling in my notebook, it was easy to see which phrases came up most often and which ones stood out as most in need of cross-examination. These are, in effect, the Top 5 excuses that inspired this book:

"It's not my fault."
"I thought the other guy was going to do it."

"I forgot."
"I didn't know."
"It's not my job."

When an employee uses any of these phrases, it implies that they are perfectly satisfied with staying where they are. They're not interested in learning. They're not interested in expanding the effort required to move up the ranks. On the contrary, they're happy to offload responsibility for any aspect of the job that might require them to think or stretch their capabilities, even in minor ways.

When employees use these phrases, it can signal anything from arrogance to skewed priorities to a lack of self-confidence. A person who says "It's not my job" is saying they don't think they're good enough to strive for the next position that might become possible if they were to learn how to solve problems that come up in their current position. A person who says "I forgot" fails to understand that forgetting is rarely an excuse, and more often an indication of where a person's priorities lie. When an able-bodied person with a decent working memory forgets something that's required of them to do their job, they are telling their employer that the job doesn't matter. And when they say "I didn't know," they are indicating that they didn't take the time or the trouble to know what needed to be known.

My hope for this book is that it finds its intended audience. If you're an employer, I hope this book helps you understand employees a little better, and gives you some new tools for encouraging people to ask more of themselves. And if you're an employee who has ever uttered any of these phrases, I hope you'll welcome the perspective of a business owner who has heard every excuse under the sun. If you truly want to get ahead, this book will help you see phrases like the ones in this Top 5 list for what they are: obstacles to your own progress. Sometimes, the first step in moving ahead is to change the way we speak. Words have power, and any of us can do well to banish any phrases that are subtly holding us back.

I have no illusions about this book being a quick fix for every ill in the workplace. Nor do I imagine that every person who picks it up will have their outlook and their life improved. People have to want to change, and be ready to receive the information that comes their way. I've been around long enough to know that many people just want to remain where they are, doing a basic job, without the complications that go along with advancement. I've met plenty of people who don't foresee any world-shattering benefits coming their way, should they try to adjust their method of operation or modify their daily maneuvers. So, they ask, why bother injecting so-called business morals or the keys to a more functional life into their routine? For those who truly want to stay where they are, this book may do nothing. But for anyone who has a spark of ambition in them, this book may just offer the honest reckoning they need.

To begin, I'd like to tell a story about an acquaintance whose self-defeating style can serve as a cautionary tale for anyone who tends to give in to their negative side. This is the first of several profiles that I draw on to help illustrate the themes of this book. The names and some of the details of each story have been changed in order to protect the parties in question.

Jerome's story

Jerome, an old acquaintance, is a prime example of someone who acknowledges that his daily habits and routines are in need of serious reform, but who can't seem to change. Like Eeyore in *Winnie the Pooh*, he radiates sadness and disappointment. Every conversation with him involves a detour into the crushing defeats and disappointments that have dominated his life. He almost seems programmed to involve the listener in flashbacks to the many intense and damaging occurrences of his past. His years of marital bliss ultimately became an agony and a misery for him. His second marriage failed almost immediately after the honeymoon because he overheard his new wife tell a friend their marriage was a union of convenience: he had the money, she had the looks. Every relationship since then has collapsed, mainly due to lack of trust on his part. His above-average career earnings turned into scanty benefits after only a few years of operating as the sole owner of his company. And the misery doesn't stop there. People who he thought were his friends have betrayed him repeatedly. His closest friend guided him towards bad investments. In short, Jerome's life has been a tragedy wrapped in a country song.

Remarkably, for someone who once achieved a fairly high position in business, he can't seem to get out of his own way, and he comes across as someone who is determined not to change. Any and all suggestions for a new strategy are met with resistance. Any attempt to engage him in conversation about his own conduct brings on a litany of excuses. He'll say: "But…I was acting in good faith," or, "But…every step I took was according to the rules," or, "But…I trusted and believed in people," or "But…I didn't know the marriage was taking a flip for the worst."

Like a lot of people who can't accept responsibility, he blames his misfortunes on "bad luck." It's bad luck that every woman he has married or dated ended up leaving in frustration. It's bad luck that his businesses failed and his housing situation remains insecure. It's bad luck that he has such terrible friends. According to Jerome, none of his misfortunes have anything to do with him, or his choices, or his approach to life. Luck, good or bad, is an external force, and his attempts to influence it come to nothing. He somehow failed to learn the crucial lesson that luck can only take us so far, and that the rest is up to us.

One of the first things Jerome needs to do is to stop dwelling on the past and concentrate on the present and on the opportunities that are still available to him as long as he is still drawing breath. There comes a point in all of our lives when we're old enough for wisdom and not too old for soaring merit. Still, Jerome cannot accept that he needs to take the next step in eliminating what he cannot fix so he can move on to figure out what he wants out of life and what he ultimately hopes to accomplish. On several occasions, he has quietly admitted that his willingness to make changes is hampered by the feeling that in the past, each time he thought he had taken the proper steps to put a plan into motion, it turned out to be the wrong decision. At times I've considered offering advice. I've wanted to remind him that everything in our past can be harvested as a learning experience to improve the present. I wanted to suggest that he move forward confidently, believing that the future can be better than the past. But I never found the right time to say my piece.

Of course, Jerome is not alone. The world is full of people who can't seem to help themselves, and who view their misfortunes as a matter of luck rather than strategy, effort, or reasoned calculations. It's hard for such people to even understand their role in making avoidable mistakes, taking inappropriate action, or using bad judgment. The way people talk about their repeated failures and disappointments tells you a great deal about how they view their own ability or inability to direct their life. While some people can hardly speak about their tendency to trip over the same obstacles, others talk and talk about each failed venture, and often seem to want to convince themselves and others that they are victims rather than the agents of their own misfortune.

I have long wondered what it is that causes some people to veer off in such a fruitless direction. One strikingly common misstep people make when trying to communicate ideas is to substitute tone for content, or attitude for evidence. Such people try to dazzle the listener by pouring out a few short sentences spoken in an affirmative or authoritative tone but offer no details or proof to back their claims. How I cringe when those moments come knocking on my door!

When people make assertions without any attempt to back them up, it feels, to me, as a listener, like I'm being handed a bouquet of roses only to find out that they're made of plastic. Or like I've just been given a book with an interesting cover but the content is a bunch of empty pages. During these exchanges, I tend to feel like a caged bird, and spend the whole conversation wishing for an escape. I often want to interrupt the person and draw their attention to better ways of communicating, but I also understand the danger, and the futility, in most cases, of offering unsolicited advice. The reality is that those of us who are preoccupied with good communication and who are eager to help others improve may well have to step back and accept that our efforts are not always welcome. Experience has shown me that pushing my agenda only serves to make me look intrusive when the advice is uninvited. And it doesn't matter how well-versed I am on a subject or how sincere my recommendations might be; all of my good intentions can still lead to personal difficulties and misunderstandings.

Accepting that it's not within anyone's power to change people's views or directly shape employee's behaviour, I have become resigned to the fact that I can only hope for the best and prepare for the worst. By accepting this reality, I minimize my frustration and disappointment and save on therapy bills.

CHAPTER 2

CHAPTER 2

POSITIVE EMOTIONS

It's easy to get worked up and distracted when everybody around you needs something. It's even worse when all they seem to want to do is complain or have you pay attention to them. In business, to be able to lead a team, one must always remain focused on the big picture and not be too affected by anything that pulls focus from those larger goals. For that reason, a leader may not be liked by everyone all the time, but if they allow trivialities to get in the way of their original objectives in order to be accepted by their members, it could well result in a loss of focus and diminished performance. This can lead to missed opportunities and reduced productivity, and can cause the organization to fall short on its anticipated progress.

Some of these missed opportunities and threats to progress come about specifically as a result of *how we think* about the things that happen to us and the people who surround us every day. One of the quickest ways to invite trouble into your business is to be the sort of person who allows negative thoughts to creep into your consciousness and overpower positive ones.

Rose Catalano

Neuroscientists like Rick Hanson call this the "negative bias," and say it's a natural product of our evolutionary need to focus more on threats to survival than on easy or pleasurable experiences. For this reason, people naturally give more weight to the negative than to the positive. But Hanson and others have argued that there are practical things we can all do to fight that tendency, and that even a little bit of success in this area can pay enormous dividends. The strategies are simple but effective, and they boil down to cultivating happiness.

Hanson argues that people should practice happiness training as a kind of meditative technique. One way to do this is to think of a past pain, then "bring in" a happy thought about something that went well, and try to keep both thoughts running at the same time, with the pain in the background and the happy thought in the foreground. It takes work to focus on pleasurable experiences and feelings, but with practice, we can develop the habit of downplaying old slights and other sources of pain just by layering conscious positivity on top of those memories. With time, the brain becomes more used to positive thoughts, and gives less weight to negative ones. According to Rick Hanson, strategies like this can rewire the brain to make us happier, kinder, and more peaceful.

To the extent that all of these qualities can contribute to improved performance in other areas of life, including business, working to overcome the brain's natural "negative bias," can be achieved by dwelling on the positive and really allowing ourselves to feel positive emotions, can actually re-program our brains for success.

The Two P's: Persistence and Purpose

Positive thinking also helps us cultivate two very important features: persistence and purpose.

Dwelling on the positive won't get you very far without persistence. This is the "grit" factor, and it's an incredibly important part of any success story. Far too many of us are quick to give up on a mission as soon as we encounter resistance or feel like we're a little off our game. It's easy to forget that success depends on cultivating the ability to *work through discomfort, overcome obstacles,* and *keep moving forward*, no matter how difficult a task may be, or how long it may take us to get it right.

Of course, work — real work, flooded with conscious strategy and geared to obtaining results — is hard! That's why we avoid it! But if you can learn to think of temporary discomfort as an acceptable price to pay for the pleasures of achievement, you can learn to push through the tendency to recoil from effort.

In order to build up grit and perseverance, it helps to identify your purpose in life and take steps to truly connect with that purpose. By that I mean that your purpose should be so tied in to who you are that you wake up in the morning thinking about it — without any sense of obligation — and you feel excited to get to work on whatever it is that will bring you closer to fulfilling that purpose.

Purpose is what motivates us to strive toward our goals. Purpose lends meaning to our lives and empowers us to do excellent work. It is the way we live our life, the manner in which we try to improve ourselves, and how we help others, that determines our contribution in life. The

Russian philosopher and journalist Fyodor Dostoyevsky once said: "The mystery of human existence lies not in just staying alive, but in finding something to live for."

As we make our way through the different stages of life, we may be fortunate enough to meet people who can teach us how to expand our personal knowledge and become more proficient at business. Such a person may even help us to connect with our purpose and develop our capacity for hard work and focused strategizing. It's important to take advantage of these opportunities. Look for mentors, recognize them when they cross your path, and grab every chance to learn from them. Watch them, and pay special attention to how they address challenging issues that get in their way. Then, as you grow and become more successful, you can think about returning the favour by mentoring others.

Root causes and subjective questions

All of the questions I've raised so far have to do with much more than business. When it comes down to it, purpose, persistence, grit, and openness to learning are all existential considerations. The key question everyone faces is one of *how to be*. And when obstacles arise time after time, that question becomes: what's stopping each of us from figuring out how to be our best self?

Of course, a question so large can have many possible answers. One of those may have to do with how purpose has been defined. When purpose is defined too narrowly, such as only in relation to social status, money, or zero-sum ideas about winning vs. losing, then purpose becomes cut off from larger values, and a person can easily drift away from meaningful engagement with their life's purpose.

When I think about the root causes of all of the problems I have described so far, I often wonder about the role played by family, schools, and the church in shaping people's value systems from an early age. I wonder how well these institutions are functioning, when so many people have no sense of a higher purpose and are wandering aimlessly through their own lives, often doing substandard work in jobs that entail very little responsibility.

Could the education system be failing to fulfill students' needs? Has parenting become an incomplete mission? Perhaps employers are failing to take the time needed to properly train, inspire, and guide their staff. Or maybe religion is not playing its part in helping people manage their values and discover their purpose.

Whatever the causes, my fear is that we may be well on our way to becoming a society that's losing the philosophical understanding of our true worth and our responsibility as adults. Who is guiding whom in the process of becoming responsible individuals and citizens with an insatiable hunger to learn, to do exemplary work, and to conduct ourselves in commendable ways?

And who will tell the truth about where we are on this slippery slope? Is anyone ready to explain why tactless behaviour and unsavoury speech are, A.) so distressingly common today, and B.) the source of such consistently terrible results? Who will steer us away from meaningless, self-defeating patterns in the workplace, like an employee saying "I didn't know" or "It's not my fault," and thinking that the case should be closed? Are we so timid that we can't even point to these behaviours and describe what's happening?

I think about the bigger picture, and I wonder if we, as a society, have any idea (or even want to begin to grasp) what's at stake in continuing to foster a culture where large numbers of people go through life dodging responsibility. How is the current state of affairs going to help us grasp the meaning of climate and cultural change, religious conflicts, poverty, inequality, the need for government transparency, and the benefit of security and social stability?

Courtney Lynch, an ex-Marine Corps Officer known for designing and delivering development progress that drives results, made the following statement: "Leaders inspire accountability through their ability to accept responsibility before they place blame."

These days, it's not uncommon to hear senior administrators and decision-makers say that they're facing non-stop opposition from within and outside their organizations. This kind of operational scrutiny can be paralyzing, and can make some corporate leaders consider abandoning their mission. And yet I think it's safe to say that most leaders and organizers are hungry for positive change and are willing to work for it. They want to see a larger audience enjoy the benefits that can be derived from more civil and productive exchanges, in both a business and a personal setting.

My experience in business has taught me that even when we are given ample opportunity to think aloud and express ourselves clearly on contentious issues, many of us fumble and say the wrong thing. Maybe we're not aware that there are other ways to broach a subject. Or, we do know how to address a situation, but we can't find the right words. Phrases such as "I didn't know," or "it's not my fault," or "I thought the other guy was going to take care of it," attest to this confusion. All of these phrases are really just ways of admitting that it's easier to spout empty words than to take action or push oneself to learn and become responsible for one's own actions in the workplace, and in everyday life.

I recognize this *modus operandi* quite well. In fact, these scenarios flash before my eyes and ring in my ears at the most inopportune times of the day and even creep up in my sleep, causing me nightmares. What those exculpatory words have in common is that they're often spoken with absolute assurance— so much so that one would think they were listening to a religious song of praise instead of a litany of excuses for poor judgment or a failure to take responsibility.

By communicating rubbish at work or at home, we can easily court dysfunction in all areas of life. Poor communication has a corrosive effect in every setting where it becomes the norm. It erodes trust and confidence, creates misunderstandings, and eats away at institutions from within, leading to inertia and apathy. It's easy for poor communication to tip the scales by making difficult situations in the workplace and at home even harder to rise above than they would be otherwise.

Self-Confidence and Communication
Many of the problems I've alluded to so far come back to self-confidence. Self-confident people tend to

communicate clearly and productively because they have nothing to hide. They believe in themselves and in their capacity to solve problems that come up in the workplace or at home. Communication is easy because there is little or no logical discrepancy, no hiding from truth or responsibility, and no need to invent or dissemble. At the other end of the spectrum, a lack of self-confidence is almost always present when communication goes off the rails.

People in this latter group often compensate for a lack of self-confidence with bravado. They have mastered communication just well enough to give others the impression that they're very sure of themselves, even when we're not. Through feigned self-confidence, people assure themselves and others that they're capable of defeating any problem as it arises. I can't count the number of times I've witnessed doubt masquerading as excessive confidence. But people who cultivate the *illusion* of self-confidence without working on the conditions that allow for real self-confidence to flourish are only creating barriers to their own happiness and success.

Real self-confidence is one of the most powerful assets anyone can possess, and should not be confused with excessive self-love or self-praise. To operate with true conviction, whether at home, work or play, requires knowledge and a sense of purpose. One of the best things you can do to improve your life and your ability to communicate with others is to look closely at all of the factors that affect your self-confidence and take steps to feel better about yourself on a day-to-day basis. Have you done everything possible to maximize your skills and knowledge for the benefit of yourself, your business, and your family and your community? Have you made the most of every opportunity that you've been given? If not, what more could you do in order to live up to your potential? True self-confidence radiates from a person who is being useful, who knows their job and does it well, who accepts responsibility at work and at home, and who has a clear conscience.

Managing Conflict in the Workplace

Conflict is an unavoidable part of life, and can be found in every setting, from families to businesses and other institutions. Wherever there are people, there is going to be conflict. This is because opinions, communication styles, and beliefs differ, and wherever there are differences, there will be disagreements. Conflict can hurt people's feelings and can push people and their opinions onto the sidelines. As a result, most of us prefer to avoid it. But conflict can also be productive, as long as it is managed well, through civil discussions, with respect for all involved. Conflict can set consequences in motion, but it can also yield benefits.

I agree with Mahatma Gandhi that, "It is wrong and immoral to seek to escape the consequences of one's acts." Everything we say and do has consequences for ourselves and others within our circle. Most of our actions are interconnected, like waves in the ocean. And if we choose wisely, we can often use the consequences of our actions to our advantage. Often it is only by facing consequences that we learn to become more skilled and proficient with what we do and say. Consequences can throw us a lifeline and lead to enlightenment when we're caught splashing around in the deep waters of confusion.

In our vast and diversified world, consequences are bound to be waiting for us in business and in life. If we can keep that calculation wedged in the back of our minds, we can find the courage to keep trying to project our ideas and actions in the most favourable light.

Inspiration (and the perils of faking it)

Managing consequences and turning them to your advantage becomes possible when you learn how to tap into inspiration. Inspiration heightens interest and can turn an unlikely proposition into a real possibility. Moreover, it can't be faked. You can't make yourself look like an inspired or inspiring business leader by constantly checking your watch or your cell phone, racing around between Very Important Meetings, looking tense and overworked, or squinting like a great leader having big thoughts. All of these pretensions only make a person look ridiculous and out of control. True inspiration yields a calm, methodical approach and produces results.

Feigning importance won't get us onto some exclusive list of executives. And why would you want to be on that list in the first place? Being in a leadership or executive position sounds like a person has reached a high point in their career, but in truth, what it really means is that the person has taken on a lot more work and a load of extra responsibilities. That position not only requires the individual to be the main person to solve problems, but it also takes tremendous skill and a capacity for hard work. One needs to be organized, energetic, and capable of motivating employees. One also needs to be quick-witted enough to keep up with daily demands and thick-skinned enough to weather inevitable criticism. To be the boss, one needs to have big shoulders for assistants to cry on. The job requires a rare mixture of empathy and unrelenting drive. And the life of an executive officer can be lonely. They wake up every day with hopes of achieving their goals, but they also know that their day may end well after the sun sets, after everyone else has left their station. The work is hard and the obstacles are many, and it's not unusual for goals to go unmet. Not everyone is cut out for this type of role, and anyone who thinks they are should take stock of these realities before deciding that their ultimate goal is to become an executive.

But if becoming an executive is really for you, there are ways to get there, and qualities worth cultivating along the way. An executive will work as hard as necessary to achieve results, often using trial-and-error to unearth the correct techniques for any given project. In a contest that is focused mostly on a healthy bottom line, the executive's steadiness is worth gold. Success may not come in one or two sittings, nor does it open the door to everyone who knocks, but cultivating steadiness will get you there sooner than almost anything else.

CHAPTER 3

THE NATURE OF DISCOURSE

Although the English language has an extraordinary number of fantastic words and phrases that lend themselves to clear and compelling communication, the way many of us use the language falls far short of its potential. Language experts tell us that there are more than a million distinct words in the English language, but that the average person only knows approximately 20,000 words (for the university-educated set, the figure rises to about 40,000). Moreover, most people have settled on using fewer than 5,000 words regularly, depending on their occupation, education, and personal interests.

For some reason, my industry (security) seems to be made up of people who get by with a lot fewer words than that. The people I've encountered in the security industry tend to use short sentences and rely heavily on body language, such as: avoiding eye contact, slouching, shrugging shoulders, crossing arms across the chest, and nodding.

Obviously, some people are more language-oriented than others. And there are other factors at play as well, including family background, socioeconomic status, and many other aspects of a person's life history. Not everyone cares about words or is willing to do the work to expand on their existing vocabulary. And there are plenty of occupations where verbal fluency is neither a requirement nor a necessary part of the job. Flooring, factory work, landscaping, and cleaning, are just a few of the essential occupations that don't require strong communication skills. In many of those jobs, one will do just fine speaking the way others speak: simply and informally.

And yet, I have never been able to understand — or accept — my own industry's preference for simple communication. While education requirements are not as high in the security business as they are in some other industries, I still consider it to be a sensitive occupation that requires strong people skills and therefore advanced communication skills. This is especially true when security for people or property fails and officers need to step in. Clear communication is vital for resolving conflict, and yet language skills are generally scarce within my industry.

At the risk of sounding like a fault-finder, I have noticed a creeping tendency for people to use fewer and fewer words and to express themselves less effectively. I've known people who have the ability to interact with a certain degree of fluency, but who are not interested in putting in the effort to utter a full sentence. I can only assume that they find the idea of communicating clearly and in depth to be a strenuous workout.

And if speech is a problem, writing is even worse. Writing things down as a means of avoiding confusion is an important part of almost any job, and yet few people master even the simplest forms of written communication. Some of this may have to do with a fear of making mistakes.

But everyone makes mistakes, and every mistake is an opportunity to learn. No one should shy away from writing because of a misplaced idea that they need to do it perfectly every time.

During my years in the security business, I have heard an enormous amount of unclear speech and read a king-sized amount of incomprehensible writing, usually in the form of written excuses and explanations for why something that needed to happen couldn't happen. I've seen it all and heard it all. I did not imagine any of it. What would grab my attention more than poor communication was the nature of the problematic occurrence. So if you're holding back from writing or speaking on the job out of a fear of being judged a poor communicator, I urge you to get over that fear and know that most employers will be understanding as long as you've taken responsibility for your actions. In most situations, *what* you have done is far more important than how you explain what you have done.

Political mumbo jumbo

Uncanny as this may seem, excuses and poorly framed explanations are not reserved only for the workplace or the home front; they're prevalent in political life, too. Bizarre excuses are so common in that third realm, in fact, that I've gathered them into a separate Hall of Shame. My favourite political excuse of all time was delivered by MP Pat Martin, the NDP (New Democratic Party) Member of Parliament from Winnipeg Centre, on February 19, 2015 as reported by Adam Frisk of Global News. When Mr. Martin was questioned about why he left his seat in the House of Commons during a voting session (a serious no-no), he blamed, of all things, his tight- fitting underwear. "I can blame it on a sale that was down at the Hudson's Bay (Company) — they had men's underwear on for half price," he explained. "I bought a bunch that was clearly too small for me and I find it difficult to sit for any length of time, Mr. Speaker." I kid you not. He actually said this.

Second place in my Hall of Shame goes to U.S. Senator Larry Craig. In 2007, Craig, a Republican senator from Idaho, was arrested for lewd conduct in an airport washroom. Reuters reported that he was caught playing footsies — literally — with the person in the next stall, who turned out to be an undercover police officer. According to Sgt. Dave Karsnia's arrest report, Mr. Craig's basic defense for his action was that he was "a wide guy" and that his foot may have accidentally touched the officer's foot. Craig later pled guilty to a misdemeanor charge of disorderly conduct, all the while trying to convince the court of public opinion that he had done nothing wrong. Apparently, Senator Craig's questionable behavior did not end with the bathroom issue. According to an article by the *Washington Post*, he was also found at fault for misspending campaign money when he desperately tried to retract his guilty plea, which cost him a few hundred thousand dollars. In 2014, a federal judge ordered him to pay a fine of $242,000 for misusing campaign funds.

Craig's verbal gymnastics in this case qualify him as a blunderer and a hypocrite.

Another fine example of a powerful person offering the world a ridiculous excuse for his behaviour comes from Mark Sanford, the former governor of South Carolina. In 2009, Sanford flew to Argentina to enjoy a week-long rendezvous with his Argentinean lover, Maria Chapur. To explain his absence from the office, he told his staff he was "hiking the Appalachian Trail." What a weird tactic! Why would he choose to reference that trail? The Appalachian Trail is known to be a grueling and demanding journey and most of it is agonizingly difficult. The place Governor Sanford was heading for was nothing of the sort. He was on his way to a pre-planned retreat spurred by impulsiveness and hormonal urges. In the end, his dishonesty caused him to resign as Chair of the Republican Governors' Association, although he was able to finish his second term as governor, and he later reclaimed his old seat in Congress and served in the House of Representatives from 2013 to 2019. It's fair to say that Mark Sanford paid a relatively small price for his infidelity. And yet his marriage ended, as did the affair with the Argentinian woman who he called his "soul mate." I often wonder if, in retrospect, he would have done things differently. And I'm intrigued by his quirky lie about his whereabouts. Why the Appalachian Trail? I doubt even Mark Sanford can explain that peculiar choice.

Keeping a sense of humour

These three politicians are hardly alone. It's a sad truth of the human race that people often lie to explain away poor judgment and bad choices. The reality is that at any point in our lives, especially in business, sticky situations can derail us from the truth and even cause us to temporarily lose our grip on reality.

Most of the time, when I find myself facing less than believable stories, I do my best to remain enthusiastic, optimistic, and open-minded. I find that the best approach to situations like this is to keep one's sense of humour alive. Making light of a situation, regardless of how heavy it feels, is an indispensable tool in my survival kit. Keeping a sense of humour has the potential to help improve my leadership skills and, at the same time, allows me to blow off steam. Besides, I read an article that said laughter in an office environment can facilitate weight loss. Well, if that's the case, I have no qualms playing along with this method of exercising, especially when it yields such clear benefits.

More than thirty years ago, Norman Cousins, an American political journalist, published an article in the *New England Journal of Medicine* exploring the potential health benefits of laughter. Adults tend to laugh about four hundred times a day, and each hundred laughs uses up about the same number of calories you would burn by walking on a treadmill for ten minutes. Furthermore, a Mayo Clinic article published in June 2011 states that laughter soothes tension, stimulates circulation, and can ease pain by increasing the body's capacity to fend off stress. To me, these insights are nothing short of amazing. So I try to keep the office atmosphere light and make sure that there's plenty of room for laughter. But this doesn't mean that anything goes. Far from it. I'm still going to speak out when I notice waste and inefficiency, which are two of the key culprits behind inadequate business growth. Indifference to economic risk and a poor work ethic have always strained my psyche. To see people frittering away time and resources sets my teeth on edge. Wasting time may be good for one thing: it gives the brain a rest. But, too much rest and a constant do-nothing attitude will lead to loss of direct value. And that is no laughing matter!

Fritterers will fritter

One day, as I was heading down to the main floor of the office to discuss the next quarter's financial forecast with the operation manager, I saw two employees standing next to the photocopier. They seemed to be engaged in intense conversation, and as I approached, I could hear that they were discussing the latest political polls. They were so caught up in what they were saying that I don't think they even noticed me slowly making my way past them. Neither one of them had time to lift their eyes and acknowledge my presence. Twenty-five minutes later, I returned to my office and had to do a double-take when I saw the same two employees still standing in the exact same spot, now talking about their favourite football star. These two gentlemen were not giving their minds a badly needed rest from the trials of the work day.

They were not recharging their batteries in order to pour it on during the rest of the work day. They were standing around on company time, completely ignoring their responsibilities, right under their employer's nose.

My disappointment grew as I watched them squander paid work time in ways that provided no value to the company.

As disturbing as it was to watch this scene, I take some solace in knowing that I'm not alone in wishing that employees would stop wasting company time. *Salary. com* and *Harris Poll for Career Builders* have conducted many studies on this subject, and have shown that this type of issue affects industries and companies of all types and sizes. Judging by the absurd situations my colleagues have had to deal with over the years, I think my business has fared pretty well in comparison. I say this because so far, unlike those colleagues, I have not experienced the distress of catching an employee hiding in the warehouse between stacks of boxes in order to grab an afternoon nap. Nor have I lost a competitive edge because a disloyal employee disclosed the company's secret with regards to our price structure.

Value added

These and other true stories boggle the mind. Moreover, situations like this can sometimes get a disproportionate amount of attention from business owners who feel their company's worth is slipping away every time an employee wastes time and resources. But it's important to remember that we cannot measure productivity or service quality based solely on one, two, three, or even a hundred people's performance. And it's equally important to recognize and appreciate the value added by consistent performers within the workplace.

As someone who has employed many people during my thirty years in business, I'm eternally grateful for those employees who understand and accept responsibility and who add value to the company through steady, consistent and conscientious productivity. These workplace stars are always ready to learn and grow. They view their work as meaningful and important, and not just as a job. They make wise decisions about company spending and they keep their wits about them in ways that help to prevent losses and ensure long-term company growth. I'm always so much more relaxed when I know that I have staff members on board who can, and will, approach a task with the same standards I expect of myself.

I also owe these employees my gratitude for keeping me in the loop when any unpleasant news comes our way. In business, it's important to ensure that all news, good or bad, is brought to the surface and dealt with promptly, if only to minimize the potential for future damage to the company. Even though many company owners dislike sorting through the trivialities of daily operational hits-or-misses, I find it worthwhile not to close my eyes to the stringent demands made on our field staff, and in particular on the security guards. There are times when the interaction between the service staff and the customers can get a little testy, and it's essential that management be mindful of the challenges these employees may face at any given moment.

We also need to be cognizant of an uptick in incidents that can test employees' patience. As an example: a patrol guard was once accused of not doing his job because the site manager could not see him patrolling the underground parking area on camera #11. The fact is that camera #11 was defective and not transmitting video activities. In another case, a service technician was blamed for not being experienced enough to address an intercom issue, when in reality, the site administrator could not follow programming instructions and accidentally deleted the data files. No apology was offered for either of those incidents. This kind of thing can create justified ill will, and business leaders need to guard against it. No one likes to be blamed for something that's not their fault, and when it happens, a sincere apology is in order.

People over process

In business, as in our personal space, keeping equilibrium between expectation and reality is of paramount importance. Otherwise we risk slipping beyond the point of rescue. For this reason, my management staff and I do our best to uphold our company's belief that people must come first, and be prioritized over process. To this end, we keep a close eye on our employees, and take steps to identify any conditions that might discourage the field technicians and security guards from wanting to return to work at their previously assigned posts. While no security personnel can be protected from bullying or pushback in all cases, we make every effort to safeguard our employees and allow them to do their work. A well-trained security guard can deter mischief just by standing still and radiating authority. But guards need to feel secure in their position, and we as business owners have a role to play in making sure that's the case.

In spite of the fact that security guards who are licensed for parking enforcement duty don't dress like the police, don't drive police vehicles, don't have the authority of police officers, and earn significantly less than police officers, they can still make people see red when they place a parking ticket on their windshield. Judging from their reactions, you'd think some of these drivers had just received a registered letter from their mortgage company or their spouse's divorce lawyer. Perhaps because they know they are dealing with guards rather than police, many people who receive tickets blow up at the guards. Such incendiary scenes can cause serious stress for the guards.

I've heard outrageous stories from security guards who are at the beginning of their career and who have already heard vicious insults. I clearly recall an incident with an employee who issued a violation notice to a man who was unlawfully parked in a no parking zone. When the guard called his attention to the no parking sign in front of him, the driver adamantly refused to move his vehicle. The guard's second request to move the vehicle also failed, and after a third failed attempt to persuade this driver to obey the rules, the guard gave the man a fine. Naturally, the driver went ballistic. But that wasn't the end of it. After heaping a big dose of blasphemy onto our poor, beleaguered employee, the driver decided to pull a "Full Monty," exposing himself to the poor guard, who was just as confused as you can imagine.

Obeying parking regulations is not rocket science. It may be inconvenient, but it's not complicated. So it's safe to assume that this man understood the rules and just decided to break them, even when confronted. But why? How does anyone justify that kind of behaviour? There are, of course, myriad possibilities. He could have been having a terrible day. Maybe his fiancée broke off their engagement. Maybe he lost his job, or a parent, or his house that week, and was taking his rage out on the nearest target: our employee. Maybe he suffers from a mental illness or an anger management problem. Maybe he's heading into a midlife crisis and defying parking regulations is the only way he can feel like he's in control. The root causes of defiant behaviour differ from person to person. But whatever the cause of this man's outburst, the bottom line, for us, at least, is that one of our employees was thrown a major curve ball in the course of his job that day. And this story goes to show that the stresses of being a security guard are real and pressing.

Like police officers, security guards are often misunderstood and disrespected by the public, but security guards arguably have it worse than police. As private citizens in uniform, security guards represent a certain level of authority, but their powers are limited. Some guards carry batons, and security companies that handle money often employ guards who are licensed to carry firearms. Moreover, guards can arrest and handcuff perpetrators and hand them over to the police. But it's the police who routinely carry guns, and police who decide what happens to any perpetrator that a guard arrests. As a result, security guards don't get a lot of recognition or praise for a job well done, and can even face open disdain. Take the common attitude of shoplifters, for instance. Shoplifters are of the opinion that security guards really don't pose a big threat to them. Past experiences have taught them well! They know that if they manage to outrun the guards, their actions will go unpunished. If by chance the guards are fast on their feet, they can only detain the shoplifters if they have actually witnessed them committing wrongdoing. And there is another point in these culprits' favour: they're fully aware that no one in management wants to see the guards cause a scene on their premises.

In the security industry, as in most other industries, field personnel are not the only ones to face constant challenges and scrutiny. For any company to succeed, the whole team, including administration, sales, operation, technical staff, supervisors, middle management and senior staff, must work in unison. In order to avoid unpleasant surprises, the office workforce must be fully capable of managing the field staff through any eventuality. For this to work well, upper management has to ensure the whole team is on their game. Many times, this process is rendered expedient and efficient with the help of a video surveillance system to monitor both the exterior and interior activities of the workplace. This being the strength of our company's business, our team is well aware that video data is the gold standard; it records the facts, and only the facts. Video recordings are not selective, and nor are they discriminatory. One of the most useful things a company can do to protect its workforce is to install good surveillance systems to ensure that events are captured. This provides a record of events and can often come in handy, protecting employees against complaints and false charges.

GEMSTOR
Security Service Ltd.

SECURITY GUARDS

CONCIERGE

MOBILE PATROLS

ALARM RESPONSE

GEMS
SECURITY SYSTEMS INC.

VIDEO SURVEILLANCE

ACCESS CONTROL

AUTOMATIC DOOR OPENERS

INTERCOMS

ALARM SYSTEMS

Stories from the front lines

Of course, a good in-house surveillance system can also tell you when your employees are not doing their jobs correctly.

One afternoon, I was en route to a business meeting with a longstanding customer. As I was about to leave the office, I called on John, the in-house tech, to review the office video footage from the previous night to ensure all had proceeded well and according to company regulations. The second purpose of this exercise was to ensure the night staff had followed a new set of safety and security protocols that had been implemented weeks prior.

The safety manual clearly stated that as of 8p.m., the rear and front office doors had to be kept locked. These doors were not to be opened at any point, except to grant access to authorized staff. John dutifully called up the video footage, and as it began to roll, he couldn't believe his eyes. What he found shocked him so much that he took it upon himself to review the data from two previous nights, hoping to satisfy himself that the careless incidents he was seeing were exceptions, not the norm. Sadly, that was not the case. One of the employees who covered these three late shifts had deliberately broken rule #1 and had kept the front door unlocked all night. My best guess is that by avoiding the inconvenience of having to lock and unlock the door, she could dash outside for a smoke as often as she wanted to, and the cameras would cut her some slack. Obviously, the safety regulations the company had implemented were of no concern to her. Clearly, the potential for harm to herself and others did not move her at all.

This, despite the fact that there had been recent stories about women being attacked by undesirables prowling for victims at odd hours. John was shocked to realize that this news coverage had not fazed her in the least. Perhaps she believed herself to be invincible. Maybe she thought bad things only happen to other people. Clearly, she had not even considered the possibility that she could have been raped or killed. John could hardly contain the fire in his belly to confront this co-worker about her actions. Her cavalier attitude toward safety violated everything our company stands for, while also putting her own safety and the safety of everyone else on the night shift at risk.

I believe I speak for most employers when I say that a company's prime value is the safety of its employees. In my establishment, we strive to ensure our employees stay safe and are kept informed about our required safety procedures. With that in mind, we pay close attention to any safety mishaps that happen at the office or in the field, regardless of how small they may be. But, for whatever her reason, this employee didn't care to use the resources at her disposal, nor did she feel the need to apply those safety measures in a responsible way. Why is prompting people to stay safe such a difficult task? By all accounts, the need to follow health and safety measures should be a simple concept to grasp. The consequences of poor safety can be serious. Furthermore, mishaps definitely aren't predictable. So far, I have yet to meet anyone who can put a dollar figure or an emotional worth on how much a misfortune or a fatality will cost people and companies. What is the asking price for the burden of emotional scars these days?

Suspicious of this employee's overall work ethic now, John continued to view and analyze every clip of the recorded data. As the video images rolled, dismay overtook him. After a few minutes of observation, all he could do was stand there in disbelief as he watched her entertain herself by playing video games on her device when she should have been filing site reports and paying attention to the nature and urgency of the incoming alarm calls. Unlike her, the cameras had done their job. They told an ominous story, and all he had to do was ask for it. Being of the opinion that this untrustworthy associate was intentionally failing herself, the company, and her co-workers, John decided that she needed to learn a valuable lesson. After a few moments of indecision, he copied the video footage of all three nights' proceedings onto a memory stick and personally and discreetly handed it to the human resources manager to deal with the matter accordingly.

Was this employee afraid to give her best? Was she simply not interested in bettering herself? Was she a slacker, so addicted to playing video games on her tablet that nothing else mattered? Even though I try not to brood over such sad realities, because my days are very busy with work, sometimes I find myself fascinated by the root causes of such self-destructive behaviour. It's hard for me to accept that some folks consider rules that I hold sacred to be optional at best. I wonder how such careless and chaotic people will survive out there in the world. Do they have the faintest idea how to build a solid future for themselves? Do they have a vision for their life as a whole, or are they satisfied to live in the moment, even if that gets them nowhere? If we were to come up with easy things for them to do, would that help them focus their attention? To entice such people toward self-improvement is a tall order when they don't want to help themselves. It's certainly anyone's prerogative to choose an alternative path and be satisfied to go through life with half-baked values and without having to rush around to make the most of every minute of the day. However, by pushing the pause button, a person may avoid the hard tasks and choose to do the easy stuff but, it will not move the needle very far.

Fear of change

While some of these tendencies can be chalked up to simple immaturity in younger employees, self-destructive behaviour in older employees can sometimes be traced to a fear of change. For adults of a certain age who view the past through rose-coloured glasses, it's scary to consider the possibility that their skills might be becoming obsolete. It's natural to feel alarmed when the new replaces the old, especially when change accelerates as much as it has in recent decades.

But is it rational to allow fear of the new to stifle your growth? I believe that leaving behind what you know in order to move toward what you don't know is one of the hardest, and at the same time potentially one of the most rewarding things anyone can do. And yet many people dread change, and find it hard to adapt, even when their future is at stake. The same feelings of dread also occur when we find ourselves wishing for an easy escape from complex problems.

Regrettably, there are very few easy solutions to any of the real problems that arise in business. It is up to each of us to set goals and commit to them, live in the present, have ambitions for tomorrow, tip our hat to good values, keep our focus on what we do, and do it well. Things may not always turn out the way we want, but with continued effort, a little resourcefulness, and unwavering dedication, we'll find our way.

Business Ethics

In 2016, Todd Pheifer published a book called *Business Ethics: The search for an Elusive Idea*. In it, he connects business success with larger ideas about morality, and argues that "Effective decision making, policy construction, and organizational management are about developing an understanding of the principles that guide our daily living."

Pheifer's book offers practical tips to help us run our businesses more efficiently and ethically at the same time. In my opinion, he's a great connoisseur of the values and principles that can help to guide us toward success in all areas of business and life.

Fans of Pheifer's work, like myself, share his belief in the value of cultivating morality in business. His work has done a lot to influence my own thinking about business ethics, and informs much of what I say in this book.

Whether we're in a moment of crisis or in the process of administering an everyday task, how can management better prepare to deal with individuals who have no desire or no aptitude to improve, take responsibility, or tackle situations head-on? On a good day, these are the employees who only manage to complete one transaction every twenty minutes instead of every seven minutes, and then leave the office for a smoke break or to get an espresso at the corner restaurant. Their long to-do lists are apt to remain untouched for a considerable amount of time, or until they've been reminded about them a few times a day. Items that require serious attention are neatly placed at the bottom of the pile, out of sight, and they do the easiest ones first so they can feel they've accomplished something. Then they convince themselves that the remaining pile on their desk can wait to be tackled another day, when they can better weather the storm.

Solid, consistent producers work very differently. In fact, their habits are all the opposite of what I have just described. They keep organized to-do lists and tackle the most difficult items first, in order to make the best use of their time and energy early in the day. Their conduct enhances workplace productivity, and when an opportunity presents itself, they are ready and willing to share their skills with other members of the team. They are a proven commodity and often remain on their game even after the workday is done. Somehow or other, they manage to stay at their desks while they're on the job; they don't take smoke breaks because for the most part they don't smoke, and they sip tea or in-house brewed coffee while they try to squeeze maximum productivity from every shard of time.

Could it be that these dedicated team members are hard-wired to settle for nothing less than doing their best? As the old shampoo commercial goes, maybe they were born that way. Or maybe they were just lucky enough to be born into stable families, headed by parents who modeled a strong work ethic for them, who read to them, loved them, disciplined them proportionally, and encouraged them to develop good habits. Whatever the root causes of the behaviours that lead to solid, consistent, reliable employees, I am beyond grateful every day for their very existence.

Sadly, the world is populated with many people who can't, or won't, rise to this standard. Some even look down upon the level of commitment that I've just been describing. Such people are essentially pessimists; in their narrow, defeated view of the world, whatever is dreary will always be that way. And if they excel at anything, it is wasting time and opportunities. Some people believe that it's a waste of time aiming to achieve challenging goals, and that to have a happy life everyone should adopt a laissez-faire attitude. With no rules or controls in place, one can do whatever one can, whenever one can, and we'd all be free of pressure.

Slackers have tested my organization countless times, and each time, common sense has showed them the correct way. I've watched employees waste time and opportunities, without seeming to notice or care. I've watched them miss important company deadlines while stretching out their work breaks like they were testing the elasticity of a rubber band.

Inevitably, it was left up to me to clarify what is acceptable work behaviour and what isn't. In the meantime, while these employees were abusing company time, I and a few managers were keeping notes on their behaviour and storing those observations away for future use. After some thought, the management staff began to calculate how much the business was losing as a direct result of time wasted on the job. Because wastage drives me nuts, I found myself putting a dollar figure on how many uniforms, rolls of toilet paper or paper towels, cases of bottled water, and other office supplies this lost revenue would buy.

I'm certain I'm not alone in realizing that my company's bottom line has seen some damage caused by a constant trickle of wasted time and poor decision-making by less-motivated and less reliable employees. I'm sure that this has been a problem in every industry for a very long time. Wastage appears to be coming from multiple sources and is heading nowhere in particular. The real question is: Do we plan for more of the same and hope for better results, or do we ask what business owners and senior management can do to alleviate this virulent disease?

Plenty of senior staff members have puzzled over how to solve the problem of turning weak, unmotivated employees into stronger ones. Maybe we're dreaming if we think we can ever solve this issue! Then again, maybe we should tackle it from a different angle. Albert Einstein wrote that "We cannot solve our problems with the same thinking we used when we created them." If some people are inclined toward laziness and time-wasting, what kind of system changes might help them to do better? What strategies can we use to motivate people who are, by training or by nature, inclined to be unmotivated?

While I know these are the right questions to be asking, I often find myself wandering down other avenues. I wonder, perhaps fruitlessly, where the problem even originated. Who in their right mind had the audacity to create this type of uncontrolled and counterproductive behaviour? It wasn't anyone I know or any of the employees in my establishment! Did an interloper get bored one day and start devising a plan to make everyone around them less responsible, less productive, and less efficient? Does a person's dependability and accountability become irrelevant when they choose to ask "what is the minimum I can do" instead of "what can I do to prove my worth?" or "how can I contribute to this organization in a way that will benefit everyone?"

I understand, of course, that not everyone has the same luck, training, talent, or resilience as our top producers have. The world is complex and, yes, unequal, and people are subject to an extraordinary variety of circumstances that can and do influence their behaviour. I try to be understanding of the forces that might cause someone to be less efficient. But, what I truly don't understand is this: Why do so many people choose to cut themselves off from the pulley of progress?

When I first opened my business, I recall thinking about the possibility of having to address the performance of employees such as the one we assigned to the night shift. I confidently put the probable event alongside the wayward performers I had come across in my past management role in the private sector. Seemingly, no amount of experience provides adequate defense against the surprises that pop-up in a busy day in the service industry. If nothing else, this employee reinforced the notion that there are those who feel that neither the world, nor their place of work, offers them any satisfactory compensation. She is one of many people who are predisposed to disregard sound instructions because none of these directions have been fashioned by them. It's obvious that people like this have their own mission, which is, as far as I can tell, to do as little as possible. But can anyone really say that this is an effective format for anyone, anywhere, anytime?

The probable answer to any of these questions can sometime make my stomach flip, and I'm forced to accept that doing business these days has just become very costly and a whole lot harder than it should be. When I find myself in a loop, repeating the same idiocy that I've encountered so many times before, I give my head a twenty-second squeeze with both hands, and then acknowledge that I'm trapped in the same situation as many other business owners. To make the situation a little more bearable, I rely on renewed hope and fantasize about the day when we'll have a tremendous pay-off for enduring all these headaches.

Posing questions while being careful not to disrespect anyone, I ask my colleagues: What's happening to efficiency in the workplace and in the home turf? What's happening to the idea of putting in a day's worth of solid work accompanied by the appearance of gratitude and awareness?

Defining efficiency

Again and again, senior management and business owners regurgitate the same old questions, even though we're all aware that answers aren't expected anytime soon. Merriam-Webster defines efficiency as "effective operation as measured by a comparison of production with cost (as in energy, time, and money)," and as "the ratio of the *useful energy* delivered by a dynamic system to the energy supplied to it" (emphasis mine). What has happened to people's ability to generate useful energy? Why is it so hard to find people who devote every day to being as effective, dynamic, and productive as they can be?

Efficiency is a measure of productivity that determines how much we get out of a transaction in relation to how much we invest in it. As such, efficiency brings progress. To achieve progress is, again according to Merriam-Webster, "to develop to a higher, better, or more advanced stage." Progress is essential for reaching larger goals such as equality, advanced medical discoveries, economical improvements, and technological growth. However, we must be careful not to let the search for progress become a frenzied whirl of empty activity marked by non-stop work and the impulse to get places faster, without pausing to reflect on where we're heading or why.

True efficiency arises out of steady, thoughtful action toward well-understood goals. These principles can be applied to the workplace, and can help to define the habits and practices of truly efficient business leaders and employees alike. As much as possible, everyone should be striving to bring as much methodical and useful energy as they can to each day's tasks. This begins at home, with getting enough sleep and eating healthy food and avoiding drugs and excessive alcohol. Good health lays the foundation for better efficiency in every area of life, including business. Then, once we're actually on the job, we should avoid things like double-booking appointments and stretching our work days just to see how far we can go before we reach a point of personal anxiety.

Achieving efficiency

Efficiency can be achieved through varied methods and strategies. One of those involves multitasking. Anything from household chores to writing a report, charting a growth graph, researching a new product, organizing work schedules, collecting outstanding receivables or summarizing expense reports may have more than one way of getting it done. Moreover, different methods may yield different speeds and different error margins.

Here is where multitasking skills comes in. For eons, multitasking has been considered the best strategy for maneuvering through daily tasks in a manner that facilitates workflow and keeps workload manageable. However, multitasking also has its critics, and is sometimes referred to as the exact opposite of productivity. Opponents of multitasking argue that it's physically impossible, and that the attempt to multitask overburdens the brain. I agree to some extent that multitasking can be counterproductive. Depending on how many tasks are being juggled at one time, it can lead to crossed signals and dropped balls. It is also quite possible that true efficiency is more likely when we break down large tasks into smaller and more digestible ones, and do them methodically, one at a time. Even so, life has a way of making us multitask whether we want to or not. And if we opt to avoid that method of operation, we may not get our desired results on time, or at all. So, by all means, multitask, but remember to take breaks, as needed, in order to stay fresh. Our brains can only handle so much. We're not computers; we can't absorb and filter information indefinitely, or run multiple applications at once for extended lengths of time. In fact, pushing ourselves to the point of overload is counterproductive, and will often cause the brain to freeze up or switch to fight mode. Either of those states can easily defeat the purpose of multitasking in the first place, leaving us depleted, distracted, and unable to achieve results.

When our strength has been depleted, we might find that we are barely managing to scratch the surface of what we needed to get done. Filtering through all of the things that disrupt our daily progress does not guarantee that we'll end up with enough quality time to take care of high-priority tasks. All of this is inevitable because paperwork and problematic situations will constantly find their way to our desk or our residence. That's when we need to take a deep breath and accept that our time is not our own. We get up bright and early each morning and head to work with the objective to get things done as effectively as we can, but things don't always pan out that way.

We can also make room to acknowledge that for everything we do, there's the possibility it could be done better, more quickly, and at a lower cost. Sometimes, all we need to do to achieve top-tier results is to take a step back, look at the big picture, and use the available resources as efficiently as possible. Other times, conquering efficiency is as easy as reaching out to our supervisor for guidance. Then, there may be those days when we're just not as sharp as usual, and may need someone to point us in the right direction. Sometimes, all that's needed is a tip or a small clue from a fresh set of eyes.

It can be tempting to define an efficient industry as one that is well-equipped to serve the public by following rules and operating at a very competitive level. In theory, this sounds good, but in reality, it only tells part of the story. It would be grand to see this same methodology be applied to the general labour market so that the conditions of an individual or a business would be enhanced without compromising those of others. Such an environment would entice business owners to manage their operations in a more generous manner. They could pay employees a better wage, encourage employees to expand their horizons (for example, through opportunities to offer their operational thoughts and ideas, improve adaptation to market changes, and inspire customers with new product and ideas), and donate more to charitable causes. And there would be other spinoff effects throughout society. Companies could collaborate more often, for the good of everyone. People could share expertise and work together to produce goods more proficiently. This would open the door to better goods and services and more economical prices. Gains would be monitored and documented every day, according to metrics that measure both quantity and quality. Such a collaborative environment would help us scan the commercial and industrial perimeters for any upcoming modernized variations, analyze global trends, and reflect carefully and clearly on the fitness of our goals.

This can be good for businesses as well as the societies in which they operate.

The alternative: competition and 'intrigue'

In the absence of such perfect conditions, companies have to make do with positioning themselves in a highly competitive environment. To gain an edge within that setting, companies must not only refine their products and services but also become innovative on the marketing side, employing strategic and creative methods in order to go after their market share.

One effective component of many contemporary marketing campaigns is intrigue. Intrigue makes the brain act like a whirlpool — it sucks in whatever we want to learn or know more about. In the business world, even when we're in the thick of things, management will occasionally decide to give "intrigue advertising" a toss of the coin. This approach runs contrary to standard or automated advertising method. It combines digital communication techniques with old-fashioned methods based on face-to-face contact and personal service. Intrigue advertising uses multiple streams of advertising in order to determine the best rate of returns.

Today, people are more prone to be intrigued by human interaction than by emails or direct mail advertising. A report by Al DiCroce, posted on October 15, 2020 in TRIB Total Media, stated that the rate of returns from direct mail advertising is only three to four percent, while using only email adverting produces returns of one percent, and display ads average .3 percent returns. UviaUS, a business experimental marketing company, also suggests that intrigue advertising is the new map for business development. A well-orchestrated sales pitch is one that combines the slickness of digital marketing with a personal touch. Done right, this type of approach can give a prospect the perception that they're being contacted because they qualify as a first-rate company. That personalized message helps the sales team evaluate the buyer's real interest. Once the approach has been humanized, an invitation to showcase the company's product and service strengths will likely be extended. This shift in marketing technique increases the odds of turning those who were thinking about investing in your service into your company's revenue generators.

Intrigue advertising typically involves a quick hook that gets people excited about a new proposal that is then fortified with a selection of animating ideas. Moreover, in the right hands, this selling method can be highly creative. Marketing is all about bringing an organization's values to the forefront, and communicating those values to customers. We all have values and goals we deem important; they can shift a static situation and motivate a variety of purchasing behaviours, ranging from buying a new pair of shoes to choosing a sugar-free dessert.

Personal values are key to a solid marketing strategy, and when they are endorsed correctly, there is the potential that personal standards and company performance can be elevated from good to great.

Creativity in business

Creativity is the main contributor to the development of many advances, such as: the implementation and maintenance of communication services, the development of multiple means of mobile accessibility, food transportation by sea, electronic power transmission, and groundbreaking technological advances, to name a few. All of these advances have revolutionized the way we do things and the speed at which we get them done. This despite the fact that many people think that business and creativity are opposed to each other. This belief is based on the misconception that creativity always refers to art and artistry. The fact is that being creative in a business setting is the basis of improvement and stimulation that drives company growth. Progress will stall when a company sticks with the same old methods or keeps going down the same well-trodden paths it has always followed, never bringing anything new or interesting to the customers.

Business owners and upper management shouldn't panic simply because they've been introduced to a new method of tweaking daily practices. Fear of the unknown can be a debilitating enemy, and it's one that can easily stifle development. And let's not sugar-coat it: fine-tuning operations is not a quick and easy fix; it's a process. If it were easy to do, everyone would always be up to date with the latest methods of doing business and we would all be independently rich. But it helps to remember that even small modifications can enable precious time savings and add value to a company's bottom line. Now, more than ever, we need to seize opportunities to refine our methods. And while fine-tuning operations may seem like a daunting task, it becomes well worth the investment of time and/or money when it yields results.

Making adjustments to achieve greater efficiency and improve performance should not be seen as something that is only available to big companies and the well-to-do. Every company can find ways to be more efficient.

Efficiency, even in small doses, holds the power of improvement, regardless of who we are, where we come from, or where we intend to go in life. But if we can't or won't adjust our thinking, there's a good chance that our efforts will come to naught. The improvements we're looking for won't come our way through wishful thinking. To succeed in finding a viable option to improve results, it's important to remain open-minded and not allow lack of subject knowledge to make us apprehensive or interfere with our intended mission. It helps to remember that no matter where you are in life or how small your company might be, an open mind and a good day's work can produce solid and advantageous results. Working smart will remove guesswork and smooth the way to limitless accomplishments.

Procrastination

A common enemy of efficiency is simple procrastination. By most accounts, procrastination is an insidious, self-perpetuating habit that tends to be especially harmful in environments driven by deadlines. And indeed, chronic procrastination can cause no end of trouble for individuals and businesses. But not every account of this phenomenon sees it as wholly negative.

The ancient Greeks saw delayed action *(procrastination)* as a good thing because it gives people time to think about how to deal with situations and make better sense of the bits and pieces on their agenda. Furthermore, they believed that rushing to get things done may not be the way to get them done well, or to obtain meaningful results.

It's true that taking your time to tackle an issue may actually lead to innovative solutions. What's more, calculating and mulling things over for a while may lower your stress levels. If that process works for you, then make good use of it! There is no need to look for a cure to treat the delayed symptoms or to explain and re-explain our practiced stewardship as long as we think logically and achieve solid results. I think that putting in excessive time theorizing how to come up with ways to beat procrastination is a waste of productive hours because such methods rarely solve the problem. Procrastinators will do what procrastinators do; they're often good at planning, but view doing as something to be addressed in the future or, by someone else.

One way to combat excessive procrastination is to consciously try to convert dread into anticipation. This is a cognitive trick that can be harder for some than for others. Some argue that procrastination should not be labeled as a form of laziness because procrastinators are simply more risk-averse than anticipators. This, in turn, could be a matter of brain chemistry and hard-wired traits. Perhaps, the brains of procrastinators have additional power over their emotions as well as the caution button and the action mode. Anticipators, on the other hand, are skilled at managing every hour of their day, meeting deadlines, and consistently producing their quickest and best work. They're always in full swing, and frequently find that there aren't enough hours in a day to ensure everything is completed to their liking. Someone should lobby the corridors of power and put forth a motion to stretch the day from twenty-four to thirty-two hours; this might just give the doers of the world a better shot at getting to the end of their to-do lists.

It's fair to conclude that industrious people fall into the anticipator category. These dynamic individuals tend to be constantly on the move, have a positive attitude, and begin their days with a clear sense of purpose. They're guided by sheer discipline, dedication, and determination to achieve their purpose in life, and they're always looking for a way to get better results. The ones I've had the pleasure to meet and to work with all have one thing in common: they believe that hard work builds character, contributes to success, and promotes a sense of accomplishment and personal cheerfulness. Such people almost seem to thrive on stress; it makes them *more* energetic, not less. It focuses their mind, and allows them to confidently address conflicts and meet goals. Industrious people know they can't fix everything all the time, but that doesn't make them feel powerless, and nor does it make them lose their aptitude or sense of control.

Productivity

Peter Ferdinand Drucker (1909–2005) was an Austrian-born management consultant, educator, and author, whose writings helped to set to the philosophical and practical direction of modern business. He wrote many articles exploring the roots of productivity, functionality, and efficiency in business, government, and in the non-profit sector. He observed over and over again that things were not just being done wrong or poorly, but in most cases they were being done right — but unproductively. This drove him to create the formula he believed would make for "a functioning society." Drucker contended that business values are not only about profitability, but act like a scoreboard for measuring employees' alliances, customers' loyalty, and suppliers' ethics.

Peter Drucker was one of the first proponents of good business values as a better way to achieve industry goals. In his long and productive career (he wrote prolifically until his death at age 95), he published many books about appropriate management styles and about what can happen when society stops functioning. However, throughout his journey, he remained unconvinced that the dynamics of business values would ever be formalized. His career as a business strategist exploded in 1942 when his writings about politics and society at large won him a spot with one of the biggest and most influential companies of the day, General Motors. He was intrigued by the number of employees who actually knew more about the projects than their bosses did. He viewed this as a problem for the organization, and became determined to develop an effective and responsible management style that would prevent such structural break-downs in the future.

Rosabeth Moss Kanter, a professor of business at Harvard, once said of Drucker: "Peter Drucker's eyeglasses must contain crystal balls because he anticipated so many trends." Drucker was an early proponent of outsourcing as a way for companies to do what they do best and farm out the rest, and his many publications in this area helped to turn outsourcing into a major feature of the business world as of the late 1980s. But Drucker made powerful contributions in many other areas as well. He argued that good business rested on a foundation of strong communities, that a well-run business can stand among all of the other inventions of humankind, and that a company's primary responsibility is to serve its customers, not to turn a profit for profit's own sake.

I can only wonder what the world would look like, how we would communicate, and how well we could perform in our jobs and other tasks, if everyone contained within them a slightly larger share of the type of intellectual curiosity that marked Peter Drucker's career. Imagine a world of thinkers, bent on finding the best, most efficient, and most human ways of doing business. The world of commerce and human relations would be transformed. The first step towards such a utopia would be for everyone to rid themselves of resistance and self-pity, and to replace those features with curiosity. Imagine the progress that could be made, within lives and within companies, if everyone suddenly developed the inner resources to stop themselves from ever again thinking "I don't want to" or uttering the melancholy refrain of "why me?"

Digging further into the actual worth of the intangible phenomenon of wondering, I came to the conclusion that to wonder is a good thing; it is free, simple to do, and comes without self- doubt. Humans are driven by curiosity, and the ability to wonder about what could be, or to imagine what it would feel like to be a piece of a bigger whole, is one of our most precious capacities. Wonder may not be the rocket ship that propels people into the stratosphere of sudden knowledge, but it can surely act as an educational experience that helps recalibrate the entrance to reality.

CHAPTER 4

CHAPTER 4

A VISION FOR THE NEW

Aristotle believed that it was "the mark of an educated mind to be able to entertain a thought without accepting it." It's an unpromising gamble to be entertaining a thought while chasing personal beliefs. How do we know which authority to trust? Which one holds the most appropriate personal and professional ethical beliefs? The history of ideas is, of course, a never-ending story of once-dominant philosophies being contested and eventually toppled by rival frameworks. Moreover, self-interest has been a leading cause of discussion and dispute on many occasions among individuals, entrepreneurs, religious groups and world leaders.

Discussions involving these groups, when planned properly, should include social, physical, and emotional factors as the main components. In doing so, we nurture productive exchanges, especially when the intended outcome is to do good for the largest possible number of people.

If we draw our attention to institutional and communal logic, we'll discover a vastly admired performance that oftentimes promotes investing in the future while building people and making improvements for the masses. If world leaders, entrepreneurs, and religious groups see themselves as the true builders of social institutions and financial stability, it stands to reason that they should put their best foot forward and master today's ongoing challenges, encourage technical adaptations, and help elevate people's attitudes as well as corporate behaviour.

Similar to a leader's vision that inspires the get-up-and-go in others in order to achieve their dream goals, entrepreneurs bank on vision to develop a sense of direction for their business.

Without pre-judging which possibilities may or may not deliver a clear answer to what having a vision looks like for the public at large, I'm of the opinion that in general, individuals are a sizable fraction of something larger than just one person with a slim margin of ability to plan for the future with imagination and wisdom. In our own distinctive way, it's very possible that we could be motivated by different visions in order to define our objectives without the influence of biases and personal feelings. What's more, the vision for the future definitely requires all the necessary elements that facilitate economical and personal growth. In my collection of business and private precepts, I touch upon the participation and concrete actions we're prepared to take in order to achieve what we wish for. It's important to see beyond our present reality and figure out what we want to see for our company and for ourselves in the future. Although the road to this unknown destination may be rocky and full of roadblocks, and may challenge our emotional, spiritual, and financial status, I still feel it's worth making the trip.

My own philosophy about conduct within business and life can be boiled down to a few principles:

- If we think we are the only ones battling daily issues, we sure aren't looking very far and definitely not in the right direction
- If we think our job is demanding, we have not taken a closer look at what the next person is dealing with
- If we complain that managing our business finances takes a toll on us, then let's try to envision what managing the global economy must feel like
- If we think getting up in the morning is a grueling exercise, imagine what the alternative might look like…not to have another day of being
- If we complain about the pain and discomfort of a hangover, we need to figure out how to better manage its source.

I haven't yet found a socially acceptable way to say: "Stop complaining, get up, and do something useful about your situation." It's not advantageous to take a simple matter and smother it with so many complicated possibilities to the point of making life a lot more difficult than it needs to be. To say that we should adopt a simple outlook on life or in the business field does not necessarily mean we're looking for an easy way out. In my experience, the opposite can be true. By handling an operational situation with a clear-cut outlook, I can avoid unnecessary disappointment and allocate that same energy to disentangle a more complicated matter or pay attention to a long-lasting project instead.

Many people assume that if something seems simple, it can't be right, but I believe this thinking is flawed. We often look for a complicated answer to a catch-22 situation when in actuality, a simpler approach can deliver the best solution. Take a setting where differing opinions, whether business-related or of a personal nature, are being discussed. As long as the discussion is conducted in a knowledgeable, good-spirited and non-aggressive manner, I believe there is a strong possibility the end results will be encouraging and informative for both sides. The conclusion will be backed by facts and statistics and will avoid speculations. The parties involved will feel that the exercise of sharing their opinion was meaningful and engaging, and they may even offer to partake in further discussions. So, why not stop spinning our wheels hunting for difficult undertakings and complex results and keep an open mind for exciting simplicity and meaningful outcomes instead? We don't always need to take a shovel with us to clear the path to higher ground. Sometimes, we can look around and discover that we're already where we need to be. No shoveling is necessary!

On the other hand, some of us may prefer a more controlled structure. Establishing control can promote business growth, task management, and problem solving aptitude. For business owners and senior management officers, this type of approach goes hand-in-hand with critical thinking and provable reasoning. This attitude may give people the feeling that the ones in charge expect to have every project and all business goings-on addressed with maximum accuracy, so that nothing is left unsolved. They treat timing as something of the essence and do not agree with sitting still. Winning is their main driving force. People with these types of firm beliefs invariably do away with "sensitivity," especially when it comes to allowing someone's disinterest in a chosen matter to stage-manage their way to refashioning it. They see resistance to change as something to guard against in order to ensure that their thoughts and actions push far and beyond the existing conditions.

A person who has set their brain in motion toward change is one who has puzzled-out how to unleash their hidden talent and share it with others. Such a person doesn't need to fear what friends, co-workers or anyone else may think of them. Change will happen with or without their endorsement. Let's face it: without change, the world would be a boring place, and there would be nothing to look forward to.

From business to life

While most of what I'm discussing here relates to business, it is equally vital to ensure that you have a life outside of work. It is crucial to take time to cultivate meaningful connections with friends and family. Many people also gain enormous satisfaction from volunteering for nonprofit organizations. Doing so not only allows you to help others but can yield opportunities to develop skills you didn't know you had, in areas that have nothing to do with your professional life. Others expand their horizons by going into the life of the mind, for example, by writing or practicing an art form, or pursuing a hobby. Reading also qualifies as an activity that can sharpen a sense of understanding, and most of all, one should enjoy some do-nothing time to de-stress and lower the blood pressure.

Of course, it's a known fact that life outside of work doesn't always offer a haven from the stresses of a job or a career. However, each of us is the superintendent of our own life, and it's up to us to create a personal setting that will support our flourishing in the world. This will mean different things for each person. Neither the immediate community nor the whole population can assume that everyone subscribes to the same values or aspires to the same lifestyle. The universe is not made up of identical individuals, nor does everyone take stock of their life in the same way. Furthermore, not all members of a community are equal in their ability to survive and succeed.

Getting ahead in life is not easy, and to simply *think* about succeeding is not enough; the onus is on each of us to take action and not to sit on the sidelines as a reactive spectator. Like a lot of things, this is easier said than done, but it's not impossible, and there are specific strategies you can begin to incorporate as you try to become more conscious of how to live your best life, professionally and personally. Not surprisingly, given the power of words to shape thoughts and lives, many of those strategies have to do with communication.

One piece of advice that I find especially useful has to do with the balance between *how and when to assert yourself* and *how and when to leave room for others to shine*. And it goes like this: To the extent possible, do and say remarkable things that will make a positive impression, without deliberately pushing to be noticed as one of the smartest people in the room. There is an old saying that, "If you think you're the smartest person in the room, then you're in the wrong room." This can be interpreted in different ways. Not only is it important to change rooms sometimes in order to keep learning, but it can also be helpful to reevaluate what others might have to teach you in the room where you thought you were the smartest.

Everyone has gifts and wisdom to share, and if you're not learning from the people around you, there is a possibility that you're just not asking them the right questions, or speaking to them in the way that will draw out their gifts. Above all, remember that you can make an impression without stealing all of the light or the oxygen in the room. The more you learn to shine alongside others instead of trying to be the only light source in the room, the more you will find yourself in the privileged position of living and working according to a set of values that will be sustainable for you and everyone around you.

Again, it's important to zoom in on what's happening around us, call things for what they are, and not over-think inconsequential business matters, dwell on other people's political agendas (or our own), or incessantly toil over items of personal interest. At the same time, it is important to remain sensitive to the ways the money-making systems work and how the business sphere operates, as it may be a way to realize your dreams and tell your story one day.

Throughout history, labour participation has shone a light on the ethical imperatives that raise our standard of living, pave the way for workers to develop new skills, and improve the power of thought. We may not all qualify as intellectuals, but we all have an obligation to think and pay attention to the world around us in a more than superficial fashion. As someone who loves ideas, I have found myself entertaining fanciful notions of medical breakthroughs that would allow people to take a "smart pill" to boost their brain power and even add new skills to their repertoire. One can dream, but of course, even if that were to happen, the government would likely take ownership of the discovery, and mismanage this precious new gift to humankind.

Peeking under the hood

It's strange how learning about someone's biography can either enlighten the mind or cause us to doubt the person's authenticity, skill, or true contributions. We may all be familiar with individuals who have a rough and hazy life story that illustrates their previous work ethics, their interests and leisure pursuits (or lack thereof), their daily quirks, strange habits and other private life practices. I've had many moments of incredulity as I've read biographies of people who seem like major figures but who are actually insubstantial. These people are short on thoughts and facts, off on precision, and weak on technique, yet they somehow bluff their way through life, or believe they can.

Oddly enough, such people are often given more credit than they deserve. In some cases, bluffing is mistaken for talent, and the person ends up being rewarded for their shallowness, sometimes over the length of a whole career. Such people are prone to deception, and frequently cause damage to the people and institutions they're involved with. Whether it is practiced at work or at home, deceit can lead to a social disconnect, and can subtly undermine families, workplaces, and communities.

I've had occasions to converse with people from different walks of life. I've met (and hired) people who are scrupulously honest and straightforward about what they say and do, and others who will embellish or minimize the facts just to suit their needs. I've heard hope-driven stories that triggered resilience and energy, and that gave people the push they needed to keep going during hard times. Those stories created a narrative that said: "We can do this! No need to pretend!" Donna, a recently retired quality control manager, is a master at advocating for the true worth of being who we are. She's an expert at garnering interest in favour of hope and honesty, regardless of the obstacles that may get in the way. She models the philosophy that as long we believe in ourselves and our ability to stay the course, things will work out. She's a social creature whose life illustrates the importance of cultivating friendships and keeping close ties with people who you respect. Surely, Donna's example tells us, having someone to share our burden with (if and when needed) will not only lighten the load, but will also increase the potential for happiness, support and understanding.

On the flip side, I've seen people with a talent to tell stories that have a way of hijacking the neural structure of the brain and directing it to respond solely to their needs. These individuals specialize in exploiting other people's sympathies in order to ensure their own survival and career advancement. And they don't care who they hurt or how much they stretch the truth, as long as they get their way.

The value of honesty

Many people seem to believe that honesty is overrated, and that it doesn't always pay to practice it. Such people don't see any compelling reason to be truthful, helpful, or reliable. They don't feel obligated to keep their word, especially when it comes to a promise they might have made on the spur of the moment. The promise flies out easily, but follow-through is lacking.

I have even heard people make the assumption that those who are committed to keeping their word do so for no other reason than to be able to *say* that they make moral choices in their personal life and career. In essence, they seem to be saying that anyone who claims to believe in honesty is really just trying to earn points in the public sphere. Honesty, in this world view, becomes a kind of tactic played out in order to make someone feel good about themselves or to win their approval. In social media, this is the well-known sin of "virtue signaling" — pretending to hold ethical values or believe in a social cause while really just managing one's own public profile and, in the end, looking out for Number One. The suggestion that honesty might be a vital tool to build trust and open the door to supportive personal and operational exchanges is dismissed as a charade. In the face of such profound cynicism, I have to ask: How does any form of optimism or belief in self or others (let alone a higher power, or an ethical position beyond the self) take root in this type of calculation?

For those who believe that honesty is a true measure of their personal worth, it's fitting to say "they're as good as their word." Even the smallest promise has value because in general, people want to be counted on and want to avoid the viability of the relationship becoming threatened. If by chance they're unable to keep their promise for whatever reason, they get the feeling that they've failed themselves and others. At the end of the day, by and large, many of us are people pleasers and we worry about what others think of us.

Keeping hope alive

Perhaps, in due course, we all come to realize that the world will keep turning whether we make good on our professed values or not. Leaving it to "hope" to fulfill our wish is probably not going to change much for us. So far, hope by itself has not solved any of my problems at work or at home. But hope is not just a feel-good sensation; it's a true motivator, and it's central to our survival. Without hope, we have nothing. The loss of hope can bring about riveting despair, and it can even be life-threatening. When hope abandons us, we risk falling into a vicious cycle of self-pity unless and until we can somehow get hope back. Whether we're facing a difficult time at work or dealing with a complex personal situation, we must look for ways to keep hope alive, even as a tiny ember that can be reignited later when we are in a stronger position to give it oxygen and new life.

Like a lot of things, this is easier said than done, but there are strategies that anyone can follow to keep hope alive or find their way back to it when it abandons them. The key is to focus on taking small actions every day that will feed your sense of life's possibilities. This might mean calling a friend or a family member who you know will listen to you and offer support, or it might mean taking one small action every day to help you move closer to your business or professional goals.

One of the most powerful ways to reconnect with hope is to set aside a few minutes every day to write down everything that you're grateful for. Gratitude journaling has been proven to help bring positive emotions to the surface, and I highly recommend it as a way to reconnect with hope if hope ever becomes a scarce commodity in your life. Another concrete step you can take is to read stories about people anywhere in the world who have it worse than you. This can be a useful way to remind yourself of your advantages. If you can find a way to help others, even better. Giving time or money to someone less fortunate than yourself can be a good route to feeling better. It can help you get out of your own head and short-circuit self-pity. Yet another strategy is to write out an action plan for the future. Seeing the steps needed to achieve a goal written down on paper can be an effective reminder that it's often *action* rather than thought that gets us out of a hole. An action plan reminds us not to lose hope just because a daunting obstacle gets in the way, and encourages us to focus, instead, on what can and should be done to achieve the desired results.

All of this takes work, of course. It's easy to fall into a passive state of mind and wish for things that are within our grasp if only we would strive to get them, without being willing to do the work. People who do this all the time are hoping that someone else will do the heavy lifting for them. I wonder whether such people have any idea what they want out of life. Do they even have the desire to figure it out, or are they comfortable trudging through life without the hope that comes from setting clear goals and systematically figuring out how to achieve them? While this may be the shield that protects them from a drop in their social standing, the reality looks very different. By wallowing in their own passive ways, such people allow themselves to be dragged down in ways that can affect their lifestyle as well as their performance at work. Is it worth continuing on this path? I think not! Does improvement or a change of course seem to be the right thing to do? I think so.

Excuses, excuses

When I think of people who want to keep hope alive but who tend to hide behind excuses, I'm reminded of some of the underachieving sales representatives who have worked for me in the past. These employees were experts in self-sabotage. They constantly fell short on their quotas and blamed their failed attempts on a lack of available enablement tools. A common trait among these employees was their failure to take responsibility, even in situations where no one else could possibly be held to account. Nothing was ever their fault. Their poorer-than-expected performance was due to the company not adequately providing for their sales needs. Instead of voicing concerns about how they would adapt to a competitive market, they would complain that they were up against competitors who had top-of-the line devices that attracted sales like bees buzzing around a flower patch. Of course, the slump in sales had nothing to do with their sluggish attitude or their use of poor sales metrics.

In their eyes, the let-down definitely wasn't because they failed to present a compelling reason that would excite the prospective customer into thinking they just couldn't pass up the product. And yet somehow, they kept wishing for different results, while continuing to offer up excuses.

The chances of life's bounty being bestowed on them were always low, and I rarely saw them be rewarded for their lack of initiative.

It's all about words

Language is tricky, and spoken words don't always line up with people's real thoughts and emotions. However, body language never lies, and it's that puzzled and worried expression on a person's face that uncovers the whole story. Experience tells me that many people find it easier to tell themselves and others that they're "undervalued" than to accept responsibility for their lackluster performance at work. By wallowing in self-deception, they lower their own expectations for themselves and transfer blame onto their employers, their colleagues, or even their clients, or would-be clients.

As I reviewed all of the weak-willed talk I've heard over the years in preparation for writing this book, I was amazed at the variety of different forms of wishful thinking blowing out there in the wild.

You see this tendency everywhere, from someone who hopes for a promotion but does nothing to boost their performance, to the many people who complain about their hair while doing nothing to remedy the situation. The tendency to wish for things without being willing to put in the effort is widespread, and it can creep into any area of life, if you let it. Some people wish that their friends were more attentive, but never invite them out or offer anything to spark their interest. Others hope for a preferred politician to be elected, but never get involved in helping to promote that candidate. I have even seen this kind of approach when it comes to winning the lottery. If you dream about winning the lottery and never buy a ticket, you're exhibiting wishful thinking — although realistically, it might make the most sense to just work for your money and not indulge in lottery dreams in the first place, given the poor odds of striking it rich that way.

Wishful thinking can lead to feelings of detachment. The person knows that they won't achieve their goals if they avoid doing the work required to reach their objective, yet they keep avoiding it. In order to manage their own disappointment about the direction of their life, many people who are stuck in this trap convince themselves that they don't care about their goals after all. They can be quick to say things like, "*I don't give a crap about any of that!*" And maybe they *don't* care, which would mean that they need to set different goals. But often they *do* care, and are just protecting themselves from disappointment.

In my industry, as in other business sectors, all those who claim to not care seem to have one thing in common: They get caught up in their own small circle and start to think that nothing else matters. This tendency gives every indication that they're not fond of figuring out how to adapt to taxing circumstances, because, among other things, working through challenging situations requires discipline, focus, and time. It must be a deficiency of those qualities that causes the brain to be distracted from seeing the bigger picture. As a result, some hidebound employees don't see much hope for long-term gains at their place of employment, and as a consequence, they disengage, produce low-quality work, and eventually move on to another organization, hoping for a different outcome. But, as they walk into the next employer's office, they quickly find out that they have brought the same problems with them that they had in the old place. They learn that even though no organization runs perfectly, the business ideas are yet again powered by the team's energy, and that they are required to contribute. Once more, the fulfillment they were looking for begins to look like a pipe dream, because they refuse to put in the energy required to do the job well.

Entitlement

Many individuals will then call on *entitlement* to jump in and save the day. In their opinion, discipline and rules constitute an unfair infringement on their space and character. Entitlement! Yes, entitlement! There are times when bending and relaxing the rules will not be sufficient to make a person happy, even when all the checkmarks are affixed to the right boxes. Now, the "I have rights and I'm owed" litany of unwholesome demands leaves those individuals feeling cheated and blamelessly put out. What a bitter pill entitlement can turn out to be! I imagine the folks who feel they should be awarded a participation prize for showing up to work, or for completing a house chore, will see their self-worth suffer many cuts and bruises along the way. So will their days see many disappointments. Their ego will run for cover as they find out that in general, society does not see them as extraordinary citizens after all. The reality is that life doesn't always play fair, and believing otherwise may not serve us well.

On occasion, I've had sit-down talks with people who, by misfortune or poor choice, landed in this predicament. The results of the conversations differed with each individual. Take, for instance, a person who lost their job due to unsatisfactory performance, but who puts the blame squarely on their boss. They'll accuse their boss of feeling threatened by their abilities, their youth, or by their good looks, and they'll tell themselves that's why they got the short end of the stick. Although such explanations rarely turn out to contain even a grain of truth, an aggrieved ex-employee can easily convince themselves that they have been wronged in order to protect their perception of being special. Faced with a threat to their sense of self, such persons will do just about anything to avoid coming to grips with the real reason for losing the job. This puts them at a terrible disadvantage, since it all but stops them from learning anything from their experience. The entitled ego is fragile, and demands protection from reality. Made-up reasoning may provide the illusion of a moral victory in the short term, but the structure begins to crumble when a similar verdict comes from the next employer.

The truth is: anyone can, at some point in their career, become a casualty of a company's tough decision to be more efficient. Most of us will agree that losing a job can leave one feeling angry, perplexed, unappreciated and outright pissed off. Even so, filling the hole with rationalizations will not help the person come to grips with the real reasons for their termination or encourage them to do better next time. Other unhelpful coping strategies include retreating from friends and family, turning to comfort food, or binge-watching TV. None of these actions will help to restore a person's buoyancy after a hit to the ego. The only sensible approach to a job loss or another big disappointment is to stop sulking, and open yourself up to new options that may provide a better fit.

Losing control of any personal direction will bring on the risk of getting sucked into a deep hole. This is a real danger, and is to be avoided at all costs. The only way to fight disappointment is to face up to the role you played in bringing about a job loss, and set about making changes.

Obviously, I am talking about job losses that were preventable — not those that were caused by automation or other structural changes that fall outside of the employee's control. For preventable job losses, the employee will do well to look squarely at their own role in what happened. Only by doing so will they be able to ward off detachment and rekindle the hope they once had in their own ability to achieve goals. Hope fuels us. It allows us to recover from disappointments, and to recreate ourselves, as needed. Hope stops us from giving up.

A few years ago, I read a very touching poem called "Fake Identity." It was written by Louisa Coller and published online in May, 2015. Her words hit the mark, and I reproduce the poem here, exactly as it appeared, with permission from the author.

Fake Identity

My fingertips are scented iron,
I am here inside feeling so
misplaced, so irrelevant right now.

Three pairs of glasses on one
desk, two necklaces which are
beautiful, and then there is me
here, so torn up.

I'm trying every day to be
happier, but I feel like all I am
doing is, forcing out a beautiful
happy façade.

Wear the mask, play the part,
nobody needs to know your pain today.
Wear the mask, play the part,
nobody'll know your main attraction.

My friends are pretty much the only
thing, the only ones I am bothered with.
Yet now I see, it's very clear to me, that
I will need to decide my path.

Why must I pick only one
road? When I want to explore
them all, I don't want to be
forced aside, to play a
singular role this time.

Multiroling has been my key,
day #1 of false lies and screams,
I will paint a new image
of me in the clouds.

I get it that some people tend to let things slide when they get the sense that they can't catch a break in life. It's easier to hide behind an illusory self than to admit the need to change. People caught in this trap don't often see hope waving a flag, encouraging them to bridge the gap between where they are and where they want to be. Somehow, they cannot let go of the need to be the one in charge of plotting the route for their existence. When that situation arises, they'll delay looking for another place of employment, claiming they need time off to "find themselves." I've often wondered if that means they need to awaken their inner principles so they can move on to live a more authentic and purposeful life. What I'd like to know is this: when they get back to the real world, will they be better equipped to live out their new wishes and values? And by taking time to reflect on their disordered present, are they asking to be saved from themselves?

I had this conversation with my daughter Sabina not long ago, and she made the following interesting statement: "If you want something, go get it. If you need more convincing, then figure out the true blend of your strong points, and then go get it." Her expertise in Human Resources comes alive each time a subject such as this is brought up. This is how she puzzles-out that complexity: The universe is home to many people who may be missing a big piece of life's equation. Part of the problem could be attributed to a value system being under siege, and world realities not being very clear to many people within that bracket. Sabina's philosophy is that whether the crisis relates to a job loss or a relationship gone sour, if permitted, the situation can easily throw one into an identity crisis, whereby the person is told, simply, that they have lost. An attempt at refreshing and countering that phantom assault may only peek its head out when the individual finally realizes that they've lost enough and are not prepared to feed that behaviour any longer. That's the day to begin telling a different story.

High-spirited people and their stories

Most of us love stories. Telling a story is our way of transmitting the signals within our pattern. A good story, can, figuratively speaking, put us in a position to experience what it might be like to walk in another person's shoes. Telling a story is our way of conveying thoughts and experiences that make up the blueprint for our lives.

Stories told by vigorous people may very well help others to grow, learn, and become more confident. Vigorous people — or high-spirited people — are marked by a soul-stirring alertness, and manage to spread good feelings wherever they go. The high-spirited people I've had the pleasure to meet over the years have been non-prejudiced individuals, not afraid to ask questions, and not discouraged by honest mistakes. These people are dependable, proactive, resourceful, and passionate about what they do. They're experts at keeping a calm exterior, no matter what might be going on, and they know how to maintain control of their responses to people and situations. In their own way, they have an inner desire to prove who they are, and they don't treat their work as simply a job, or a means to social or economic status. But, let's not allow their placid exterior to fool us into thinking that these people are utterly passive or that they can be treated like doormats. Make no mistake; these individuals are agents with real feelings. Whatever is perceived to be easy on the exterior may not be processed so smoothly on the inside. Their configuration of worthwhile values is solid enough to suppress uncertainty, and can move forward to unbolt a new and unfamiliar gate, even though they don't know what could be waiting on the other side.

Walking into an unknown situation can be a scary adventure at the best of times, for most of us. Although new and foreign developments can evoke fear, having the courage to make new discoveries can help us determine how resourceful we are and build-in the capacity for more. As a bonus, we'll learn to rely on our smarts to tell us whether to take flight or come up with another potential solution. I'm a great believer in the need to take regular, calculated risks.

Only by doing that we can continue to learn and grow.

It takes a lot more than just thought and theory to overcome the potential perils of the unrevealed. There is a lot to worry about in the world, from financial instability to the possibility of becoming seriously injured, being unfairly judged, losing a job, or becoming critically ill. Then there are the many other forms of uncertainty that life throws our way. All of these things can make the unknown even scarier than it would be otherwise. Embracing experiences as they happen can be more emotionally healthful than drifting away from a taxing or unmapped situation to seek refuge in a less rattling atmosphere.

From a managerial point of view, it makes sense to frequently hand over new and superfluous tasks to the game-changers within the company. These are the people who have the necessary endurance to get things done. They don't complain about being unfamiliar with the subject matter, and they don't waste time worrying about getting the incorrect result for the untried exercise. They accomplish what's asked of them, and meet their obligations on time. The self-control guarantees an unwavering focal point so they can meet their targets even though they may feel the heavy burden and the fatigue brought on by being relied upon for each new opportunity or crisis.

These people are the careerists who keep pushing ahead with their extended work-week without losing eagerness or focus, regardless of whether the less productive employees become suspicious of their motives. They're not affected by the antipathy displayed by the less passionate members of staff, or by their belief that the high-fliers make them look bad in the eyes of the boss. But, as much as the dawdlers may be bitter towards the more ambitious staff, it's not unusual to see them run to safety behind the doers as soon as trouble hits. Their fear of consequences makes them run faster than the water from a waterfall onto the bed below. The moment those situations come up, a convenient and safe cover is all that's required to define who they are. Dynamo employees give it their all and accomplish what they set out to do. Their business workshops are not suspended because they don't find treats on the meeting room table, or because they're not smothered with cordialities. Similarly, they have no qualms setting their wireless devices on mute, and don't complain if the office chairs don't recline far enough. They are there for one reason: to get results.

I often wonder whether the slower moving members of the workforce could somehow trick themselves— or be tricked into being— a little more supportive of their swifter colleagues. The path to 'mount achievement' may not be smooth, but it's there for anyone who's ready to do the climb. From my point-of-view, it's the hard-working, dedicated, self-disciplined recruits who deserve endless respect and gratitude. Right or wrong, once in a while, my viewpoint can come across as disagreeable. In fact, some people might outright dislike it or oppose it altogether. But since I'm not in the habit of believing that everyone's opinion is always regulated by common sense, I tend not to get too upset by thoughts that differ from my own. Everyone's opinion matters, whether it comes accompanied by gracious sentiments or not. Therefore, if my opinion does not ring true to anyone else, it doesn't mean I can't voice my views about trivial or burdensome issues that repeatedly show up in my space. Reasoned debate promotes respect, allows us to look at things through a new set of eyes, helps one keep one's cool, and gives insight to the rigidity of one's own beliefs. When a belief is based on facts and shared with like-minded individuals, it has the ability to draw good-natured exchanges, head nods, and maybe even an occasional applause. But when that viewpoint is shared with a dissimilar crowd, the back and forth may well cause the blood pressure to rise.

Here is the amusing thing: If we were to throw an opinion out there — one that is drawn from a make-believe story —if people took to it, before long, it could quite possibly become a real occurrence and the chronicle would then take on a shape of its own. My point is simply this: Healthy viewpoints, when backed up by knowledge, can bring the right substance to the table and can boost problem-solving performance. In business, it's quite typical to find that the recruiting staff is steadily on the hunt for new hires who offer innovative ideas, can stimulate the ability to think outside the box, and bring a fresh approach and new protocols to a hard-to-fill position.

By sharing viewpoints in our everyday life, we stand to become more flexible, adaptable, and unbiased. Unfortunately, some individuals are of the opinion that whether at work or at home, something will always go wrong; therefore, their default opinion is always to expect and assume the worst. I find it hard to listen to such downbeat views for any length of time. On a few occasions, when caught travelling that one-way street, I've taken to silently raising my eyebrows as a way of expressing that I really don't want to be hung up in their gloomy worldview. Not even for a moment! All the same, I realize that disliking what I hear does not release me from my civil obligation to stay put until the venting is done. Those are the social encounters that challenge me the most. Every negative word pains me to the point of having to bite my tongue for fear of causing an unpleasant situation. I've always found it frustrating and difficult to paste on a smile and give the impression that I might agree with these defeatists or want to chime in on their pity parties. I struggle to conceal the discomfort I experience whenever I find myself within earshot of the downers of the world. Maybe one day, and I mean *maybe*, I will learn to better understand and accept the motives of these people who never let an opportunity to complain pass them by, and whose beliefs are so thoroughly fixed on the negative pole of existence.

Veronica's way

Veronica is the neighborhood crossing guard and a busybody whom I've known for many years. As the area's self-appointed guardian, she feels entitled to pry into the business of everyone who lives in the vicinity. Oblivious to boundaries, she specializes in prying, eavesdropping, poking her nose in everyone's private life, and being a match-maker when she thinks it's appropriate. She's an old hand at luring people into gloomy conversations, and her inquisitiveness often stupefies the other residents, causing them to think long and hard before answering her indelicate questions. Keeping this person at a safe distance is tricky for most of the people who reside in the area. As much as her watchful eye is appreciated, her incessant meddling and paranoia that something terrible is always about to happen more than nullifies any good will she generates.

As a people watchdog and amateur news reporter, she's never met a boundary she won't cross. Most people in the neighborhood understand her demeanor and have become very familiar with her routines. But it can be hard to tolerate her behaviour, especially when she tries to push her opinions on anyone who crosses her path. She is a verbal pugilist who never hesitates to offer her views on world affairs or people's personal lives. She has confronted almost everyone in the neighbourhood, and regularly holds forth on topics such as gun control, the state of the economy, or the allegedly poor job the younger generation is doing raising a family these days. In her day … things were kept simpler, and for that reason, life worked out much better. Young people were taught to respect adults' decisions and house rules; they revered law enforcement officers and obeyed their teachers. Her beliefs are archaic and unbending, causing many a listener to feel silent screams cut through their muscles as they attempt to prevent any signs of unease from bubbling to surface. A detection of disagreement or a phony smile would most certainly cause her to raise her voice and interrupt each time the other person tries to voice an opinion, let alone an objection.

Most of the area residents understand that all she ever wants and needs is an audience, and so they try to be sensitive to her feelings for the sake of harmony. Most of us avoid engaging her in any conversation that may last more than three minutes, for fear of ending up in a longer exchange and being tempted to set her straight on any number of issues. Such a conversation would be an assault on her role and ego, and could result in an ugly confrontation.

Although I am not a psychologist, it doesn't take a trained professional to understand that Veronica's constant complaints about society heading in the wrong direction are little more than a reflection of her own inner commotion. After enough exposure to her rants, the neighborhood has pretty much figured out that her complaints have nothing to do with trying to find a solution, and everything to do with seeking attention and/or making herself feel superior to those around her. Clearly, this woman's communication style is in need of serious realignment.

Another area that piques her interest is being in-the-know about what is going on in people's private lives. She's especially intrigued with the ins-and-outs of those who have recently lost their spouse and those who are in the process of considering downsizing their living quarters. She won't be satisfied until she finds out if the widow or widower will be looking for a new partner soon, and if so, how soon? Will that individual continue to reside at the present residence or consider condo living? What are the chances they may be contemplating moving in with their children? If they sell, how much will they gain from the sale of the property and what will they do with the extra cash?

Although Veronica's gossip shop operates a few hours a day, five days a week (Statutory Holidays excluded), I have yet to hear what her views and hopes for the future may look like. So far, I have not heard her utter any words alluding to the idea that by adapting to today's changing world, we can shine a light on tomorrow, and spread positive encouragement instead of always finding fault.

I can't help thinking that Veronica would benefit from reading the words written by Steve Maraboli, a behavioral scientist and life-changing speaker whose book, *Life, the Truth, and Being Free,* asks "How would your life be different if … You walked away from gossip and verbal defamation? Let today be the day… You speak only the good you know of other people and encourage others to do the same."

CHAPTER 5

CHAPTER 5

THE POWER OF SIMPLICITY

Henry David Thoreau, an American essayist, poet and philosopher wrote that our lives are "frittered away by detail," and urged his readers to "Simplify, simplify." The American author, politician, and ambassador Clare Boothe Luce (and not, as has been wrongly reported, Leonardo da Vinci) once said: "Simplicity is the ultimate sophistication." Albert Einstein and Confucius held to the same basic principle. "Keep it simple" was such an impactful statement that in 1939, Alcoholics Anonymous made it one of their most popular catch phrases. I would hazard a guess that this model was used to encourage its members to start by taking a simple first step: *minimizing alcohol intake.*

In today's complex world, keeping things simple can be an intriguing but elusive concept. Many of us have sacrificed simplicity on the altar of consumption, and have dedicated our lives to acquiring "toys" and other material possessions. Throughout the western world, when we say someone is living a good life, we typically mean that they're enjoying many delights such as excellent wines, artistic performances, superb cuisine, luxurious travels, and the liberty to spend money without the fear of it running out. And who on earth wouldn't want the pleasures of such a life?

But the concept of the good life was not always so narrowly tied in with consumption. Socrates and Aristotle both held that living a good life means to be a morally good person. I think we should attempt to reconnect with this definition of the term. At a minimum, we need to realize that pretending to live well because one can access pleasing experiences in life does not necessarily mean we're living a good life, especially if we cannot lay claim to living the values of honesty, loyalty, integrity, respect, friendship, and simplicity.

While many people still believe that accumulating assets and earning a big income means we've made the cut and are living a good life, the reality can be very different. Sometimes all we're doing is rushing to be the one to finish first so we can dart off to our next obligation or destination. It can be hard to identify any intrinsic value in the types of things people do so to count themselves among those living the good life. We may think we're living well, but, where and when did we lose the balance between work, play, and maintaining connections with friends, family, and community? Why is it that so many of us are seeing our to-do lists grow longer and longer while we devote less and less time to relaxation or maintaining social ties?

The answer may very well be *time*. We constantly try to outrun the clock by implementing doable agendas not only for ourselves but for office staff and family members. Some of us have become quite skillful at keeping up with car repairs, doing laundry, taking care of meals, paying the bills, raising a family, and maintaining proper personal hygiene, all in a day's waking hours. Each of these things takes time, and attempting to squeeze twelve hours' worth of obligations into a one-hour window can be crazy-making.

People's perceptions of time have changed. Anything that moves a little slower than we deem acceptable makes us feel like we're wasting time. Driving the speed limit is a thing of the past. If we go out for a walk, we're trying to squeeze in steps to win some weekly challenge or meet an exercise goal. And if we can do two things at a time, we feel like we've won a small victory, even if it would have been more effective to focus on one at a time. Rushing around all the time has become the norm for many people. The whole concept of a leisurely walk has become something of a foreign concept, available mainly to retirees, the unemployed, and the independently wealthy. The rest of us walk around with phone in hand, deep in conversation, and not really paying attention to our surroundings as we put one foot in front of the other.

We need to remind ourselves how to live in the moment. This means cultivating a new appreciation for the work we do, respecting others for who they are, and shedding some unnecessary short-sightedness about the direction our lives are taking or should be taking. Only then will we be able to live a life that doesn't require false identity. This is what I call "getting good at living a simple life." However, nothing is ever so simple. Our focus is fragmented by the force of our ego and by our disquiet over constantly wanting more— more belongings, more income, more accomplishments, more adoration, more of whatever else we have chosen to fixate on. When I lean on my business experience to think through other aspects of life, I'm convinced that true personal strength lies in being honest with yourself and others. It lies in being able to say, *It's OK if I don't know everything. It's OK if I can't get everything done as originally planned. Tomorrow, time may be a little more lenient, and I can squeeze in what I missed today.* At other times, a short walk might be what is needed to get our focus back and begin to connect the dots.

In life, no matter how we look at things, or from what angle we examine our situation, we're bound to find something that contradicts our plan for the day, or someone who perplexes our mind with their theatrics. Often the best way to deal with such obstacles is to stand back and let events unfold without trying too hard to influence them directly. A bit of "verbal aikido" can also be effective. In verbal aikido, the goal is always to receive attacks and obstacles calmly, while consciously trying to re-centre yourself, understand the other, and re-balance the relationship in a way that will allow for common ground. Why compound grief when we can change our behavior and endorse healthy thinking habits?

Why do some of us waste time desiring a more stylish wardrobe or yearning to drive a more expensive car, whether it's within our means or not? Why can't we keep things simple and focus on what really matters? Isn't life about being happy, making a difference, and feeling useful? By constantly trying to make things better for ourselves, we often end up making our lives more complex. It's not uncommon to hear of people being unable to leave their cell phone behind, even for a second, because of the obligation to be connected to whomever or whatever might need their immediate attention. When the majority of people in a society need to be on call every hour of the day, to me, that seems like a problem! Nevertheless, by leaning too heavily toward a simplistic approach to work or life, we could easily create other problems for ourselves.

Two case studies in irresponsibility

I distinctly recall an incident where one of our employees, by failing to act carefully and with sound moral judgment, not only got himself into trouble, but also put the company in a tight spot. Because he was trying very hard to complete an installation ahead of schedule, he pushed himself to work longer-than-normal days. In the afternoon of the second extended day, he became quite hungry, but didn't want to waste time leaving the site to get food. So, he improvised. He checked the manager's refrigerator for something that might be just enough to satisfy his appetite. As luck would have it, he found it! A single serving of Shepherd's pie. And since no one's name was written on it, he helped himself to half of it. Once his blood sugar was steadied, he was ready to resume work for a few more hours, then went home.

The next day, the site manager wasted no time contacting our human resources manager to report her disappointment. She couldn't believe someone had violated Rule #1: don't take what's not yours. Needless to say, her frustration was made worse by the fact that whoever took her food was not thoughtful enough to leave a note of apology along with an offer to pay for the cost of the meal. Now, HR had been looped-in to investigate the case of the partially missing meal. This complaint took us by surprise but not by alarm. Although our memory is often tested by strange episodes from some of our staff members, this one had a different flavour to it. It was a little harder to see what would have prompted him to arbitrarily make off with another person's meal. Shouldn't common sense tell us that pilfering food takes a bite out of somebody else's budget, and that such actions are not conducive to a harmonious workplace? Before all staff members were reminded of Rule #1, the guilty party quickly came forward and explained that he meant no harm and certainly didn't think he was committing a theft. He genuinely believed the Shepherd's pie was leftover food. Besides, he continued: "I didn't eat the whole thing. I just wanted to get my stomach settled until I got home for dinner."

A few days later, I was quietly reminiscing about some events that had quickly gone from simple to complicated when the true story of a larger-than-life simple case-in-point popped into my mind. I'm talking about Gloria, a distant acquaintance of mine who for many years enjoyed living a chic and easy life and who was totally sheltered from any, and I mean *any*, responsibilities. She did not have a job, nor did she want one. She did not cook, nor did she have any interest in learning how. She did not dust, did not do laundry, and definitely did not know how to mop a floor. She was convinced that the person responsible for her life and happiness was her husband. Furthermore, the financial wellbeing of the family was also her husband's domain. Gloria did not even corner the market on the most called-up qualification of a wife: lending a listening ear. Her husband ensured she was not missing out on her weekly massages; she drove the vehicle of her choice; she never missed her monthly manicure and pedicure sessions; she ate daily meals at her favourite restaurants, and smoked only filter-tipped Virginia blend Treasurer Aluminum Gold cigarettes, known as one of the most expensive brands in the world. She lacked for nothing in life, materially or otherwise. Her husband provided her with everything she asked for, as soon as she asked for it.

This was their way of life until he wasn't there anymore to pamper her to her heart's desire. When that fateful day came, she had no idea things would take a different turn, and that her living arrangements would need to be revisited. Her privileged lifestyle had left her incapable of dealing with the demands of a normal life. Now that the means of comfort were being taken away, she was totally unprepared to consent to any modification of her self-serving ways. The slightest scintilla of a suggestion that she might need to get her act together was promptly extinguished, for fear that it might bring about an unwelcome lifestyle change. Unsurprisingly, after many years of preserving her status quo, she was not about to evolve. For a few more years, there would be a large enough cash cushion for her to draw from… it would allow her to continue living life as she knew it. Her attention to her dwindling prospects was only awoken when the funds became lean and her newly straightened circumstances threatened to cramp her style.

By fluke, one afternoon, a television advertisement spoke of an innovative product that was very easy to administer; it was none other than a *CHIP reverse mortgage.* This type of loan would allow her to draw a certain percentage of money against the value of her home as long as she was eligible for it. Well, that wasn't so hard to prepare for. She wasn't required to make monthly payments against this loan; she was the sole owner of a mortgage-free house and, she was over the age of fifty-five. Qualifying was easy. The only downside was that as time passed, the equity would diminish. But, so what if it did? For Gloria, this was a good day! These brokers knew exactly what she needed to be able to continue living in her habitual fashion and not risk having the spotlight of responsibility pointing directly at her. Now, she had an agenda! Now, she could see a bright flash, like the one you might see from glowing coal. She wasted no time making phone call after phone call to the local bank. With pure determination driving her mission, she did not let up until she secured an appointment to get this plan in motion. After all, she only had to ensure she had the correct answers to a few key questions. The rest were only formalities hinging on the rules of eligibility, ease of accessing the money, and the quantity she could draw every month. None of this intrigue had anything to do with the terms of repayment or concerns over the high interest rates that can cannibalize a substantial amount of the property value. That would have been a job for her husband to figure out, if he'd been alive. Why had he not made sure all money matters were left in order, so she would be spared this upsetting and most inconvenient dilemma? Had her husband committed wealth betrayal, given that it had been decided years ago he would be the big breadwinner? They had both agreed to this arrangement without reservation, so as to avoid any possible financial spats. In the interest of fostering a healthy marriage, he would be the designated financial guru. No spoils, no pungent odours.

Instead, he'd left her to face the harsh task of figuring out what her financial income should be and not what she would like it to be. Gloria's brain was totally stirred up and was calculating numbers at a rapid pace. She had to be successful, even without knowing how many zeroes were attached to their bank balance. She would not, and could not, under any circumstance, allow herself to drop down in her living standards. Not now, not ever. She deserved better!

While that hopeful determination rang true to her, deep inside she knew this predicament did not rest solely on her late husband's shoulders. This was partly her fault for totally bowing out of their financial dealings. She should have had a vote in their money matters.

Money may not be the most important thing in the world for some people, but for Gloria, it was the source of freedom and varied lifestyle choices. Where the money came from was of no importance to her; she had elected to pass on financial literacy. But, at this time, upon re-examining her past practices, she began to look at her disinterest in their marital financial model as the root cause of her lack of skill at money management. Luckily for her, there was a substantial amount of unrestricted revenue to work with. Her next step would be to negotiate a suitable arrangement that matched the amount of money supply available to her.

Once a practical monetary allowance was agreed upon between Gloria and her banker, everything moved along according to plan. For a number of years, she continued to live quite well, while pursuing her own pleasures. She carried on spending large sums of money on clothing, cosmetics, hair care, expensive cars, and exquisite cuisine. As the years went by, this arrangement worked out very well, until it didn't. Many years elapsed before she had totally withdrawn the value of the home and was beginning to slipup on making payments for property taxes. A forlorn financial pressure was beginning to twist her arm and force her to play hardball. What was this "create a budget" suggestion the banker was talking about? What gave him the right to tell her to have a spending plan in place to cover all necessary expenses? Well, she'd show him a new and modified spending method capable of allowing her to prolong the lifestyle she was entitled to have. In a frantic effort to keep at her disposal whatever liquid cash she could squeeze in her shallow pockets and to show the banker she now had money smarts, she would take the following steps: decrease the homeowner's insurance coverage, sell household items she no longer appreciated, and withhold payments that were due to the cleaning staff and the property maintenance contractors. She would prove to the financial institution that she was quick on her feet and could come up with a solution that went beyond the average mindset. But her proposed fix was quickly revealed as a Band-Aid solution that in no way covered the gaping wound of her evolving financial situation. The banker was not impressed with her shabby plan, nor was he interested in granting an extension for a second attempt at a more concrete arrangement. Needless to say, things quickly took a turn for the worse; she was denied any further help from the bank and ordered to vacate the premises.

That day, her blue-green eyes lost their sparkle as the shock of the unexpected news came to break her character. She had depleted the piggy bank! Without any real financial smarts, she had still ventured to challenge the bank's decision. Her argument was: "It's not my fault the money ran out so soon. I didn't know I would live this long." This lady's inability to face changes and to step out of her comfort zone would have landed her on the street, if not for her son's willingness to take her in. Conveniently, her son's property had an additional dwelling unit on it - a six-hundred-square-foot casita. In Spanish, a *casita* is a "tiny house" or a small additional lodging built on a residential property alongside a single-family home. Typically, it can house one or two people.

Gloria had reached the point of no return. She felt too old to get a job, and past the point of being able to better manage her finances. It was untimely to curtail her dining at exclusive restaurants every day; it was too much to ask her to try to separate the needs from the wants; and she was too broke to dump money on luxurious vehicles. Despite all that, she had a place she could call home and no one would be so callous as to say, "I told you this would happen!" Such a phrase would certainly make her bristle as if her hair had been electrified.

Her son briefly considered bringing up the truth and reminding his mother that her downfall could have been avoided if only she'd heeded the many, many warnings she had received from the bank, and from a few friends and relatives who had been brave enough to raise concerns over the years. All the same, this was hardly the occasion for saying "I told you so." And if he had said anything, his mother would never have found the courage to thank him for cautioning her or express remorse for having failed to heed his advice. Knowing he would never hear such heartwarming sentiments, the son rose above a challenging situation and kept his feelings, and his reprimands, to himself. Moreover, he did what was needed to ensure that his mother had a smooth transition. I suspect this generous young man never knew that his pleasant demeanor made a real impression on me. The take-away here is that life goes on; we all make mistakes; no one likes being put down; and a know-it-all should add coolant to their comments in order to keep the conversations from overheating. Nonetheless, I'm of the opinion that dodging financial responsibility for any reason is not a very wise approach to life. Financial refinement is what guides us to make sound investments and expenditures as it sheds clarity on our income versus our expenses. It's through financial literacy that we learn not to spend what we don't have. Oh, and if you're in a comfortable marriage and you're letting your partner handle all of the finances, it's a good idea to get involved — before it's too late.

Mistakes and Pickles

Mahatma Gandhi once said: "Freedom is not worth having if it does not include the freedom to make mistakes." Any seasoned entrepreneur will likely agree that making mistakes and being outright wrong about a decision are part of the journey to becoming prosperous. Besides, telling someone "I told you so" can be perceived to mean that the person doing the telling is looking for acknowledgement for their smarts and foresight — and this is clearly done at the expense of the person who made the blunder.

Not all mistakes are easily fixed, however. Nor do all mistakes result in growth. When the same mistakes happen over and over again, it can be hard to recover. I'm sure we've all had moments when we've frantically called upon our brain power to help us get out of a tight spot. The Dutch describe those occurrences as "sitting in a pickle" or "in de pekel zitten." In Italian we say "sono in un sottaceto." Those are tough instances that leave us at a loss for what to say or do, and yet we know we have to do something. The result is that if we tilt toward feigned logic, the process can create a more difficult predicament and we'll feel all the more frustrated, annoyed and defeated, and we'll want to run away from it all.

Chris, the service manager of a nearby company, is a bit of an expert at being left in a pickle, especially by George, one of his senior elevator technicians. As word has it, George has excellent product knowledge and is a keen problem solver; however, he is also known for his free-flowing improvisations. Occasionally, his real service talent is obscured by the scrambled words coming out of his mouth. This is a common occurrence when he has to explain why and how his last assignment went awry. His chronicle of off-the-cuff rationalization appears to be firmly cemented in his thinking technique. After so many years of practice, he actually believes his confusion is fooling everyone involved. Perhaps he can't make out that his blunders with time management and reporting responsibilities inevitably leave the service manager in a conundrum. George obviously fails to understand the responsibilities of a service manager: taking guff from unhappy customers, relying on other staff members to make good on current instructions, prioritizing calls, being a fine and non-judgmental listener, and being tactful when dealing with the staff's flimflam. As George's list of debatable explanations goes on and on, he seems to feel confident he's making a real impact. What he fails to acknowledge is the concept that a company will only get referrals when the front-line employees are praiseworthy and portray the image of competence and teamwork. I have to wonder how anyone can say that these are merely superficial deficits which may not really alter the scale of good service quality.

There is another angle from which professional shortcomings can be overshadowed by success: through the exciting dynamics of communication. This is where we can learn about the other party's position and perspective, if only we keep an open mind. So far, I've been in on the fact that George's verbal and written approach has yet to find its way to the implementation phase. Years ago, he joined Chris's team with superior product skill, and as of today, his employer admits his expertise has kept up with his reputation. The next developmental stage is for him to improve his customer service techniques, and avoid making excuses. His focal point not only requires adjustment, but must also be readdressed to include cooperation with Chris in order to ensure customers receive timely service and product reassurance.

Embracing change

Businesses today need to remain in a constant state of flux. To resist change is to risk losing your operational edge. All organizations, whether big or small, have rules and ideologies in place, and while they may not be foolproof, they are, for the most part, designed to ensure the company's continued existence, and hopefully its success.

Of course, business owners must remain vigilant in the face of unforeseen obstacles. They must be able to rise above challenges, bounce back with renewed energy, and try again and again, modifying their approach as needed in order to prevail. I submit that if the first two tries are not victorious, it may not necessarily be due to lack of cleverness, or a faulty module, or an irate customer wreaking havoc over service attendance. The fault may well lie with elements outside of the company's control. We don't stop moving ahead because one experiment or one project went wrong, or because we witnessed operators in our niche industry dealing with one too many attempts at getting it right. One of the electronic security business's rudiments is that a service provider must showcase distinctive advantages over their competitor by providing renewed and proven forms of workmanship, people skill, product superiority, and rock-bottom pricing, even though it's general knowledge that there is no perfect way of integrating all of these elements. However, it's almost a foregone conclusion that by having a solid service design, the team will pull the company together; without it, the company will pull apart.

As Vince Lombardi once said, "Perfection is not attainable, but if we chase perfection we can catch excellence."

Like other entrepreneurs, I take note of my counterparts' experiences, if only to learn how various scenarios can play-out without harming the person or the company. At times, it's hard to accept the fact that for many security personnel, especially entry-level employees, there is little or no positive feedback given in recognition of the challenges they face on the job. Indeed, even when detailed reports are presented in easy-to-understand terms, rank and file employees receive little, if any, praise or encouragement in the wake of difficult situations. My sense is that this has something to do with social divisions. And yet I can't help wondering about the larger context for these divisions, too.

I wonder, for example, if we find ourselves at a juncture where labour, personal status, and social struggles meet. Is this a struggle that will affect each one of us, whether we're prepared for it or not? Has online communication replaced face-to-face interaction and discussion about business measures? Could this be leading to a breakdown in meaningful communication among employees and between owners and their workers? Do we have to accept this situation, or is there some way to rebel against it, and to create alternatives? At a minimum, it seems vitally important for business owners to proactively create opportunities for face-to-face communication with their employees, even when time is short and it would be more convenient to communicate online. Civility is a muscle, and everyone in an organization can help keep it well-exercised by regularly talking to each other in person. Meeting with employees also yields other benefits, from making them feel valued to providing opportunities for managers to learn about operational issues that might otherwise go unnoticed.

Enriching personal communication in the workplace also has benefits for the rest of society. The way things are structured today, with everybody in their silos, texting and emailing each other constantly, and being available all the times, is unsustainable and unhealthy. I fear that the hard-working citizens of the world are letting their lives slip away. It is all too easy to allow work and impersonal communication to take over your life, to the point where the spirit is spooked and wisdom is reduced to a numb feeling of emptiness.

Communication is an art, and it's one that I fear is being lost, or at least distorted beyond all recognition. It seems that even the effort to speak less or to communicate in simpler terms, still doesn't guarantee that anyone will listen. Has communicating with a family member, a friend, an employee or a co-worker really become so complicated these days? Maybe current ways of communicating are just a comic imitation of something else. Maybe the new ways we have of connecting and communicating with each other are only temporary. After all, language and communication change all the time. I do sometimes think that we're facing a kind of slapstick imitation of the type of verbal or written communication style that used to help people build confidence, determination, and precision.

I'd venture to say that if we find the correct answers to our questions, it would give credence to what we believe to be right, reason to our deeds, and a voice to our body language. And that, I think, would be quite OK for most of us.

The term "OK" has been attributed by some historians to seventh US President Andrew Jackson's poor spelling of the term "all correct," which he rendered as "oll korrect." This abbreviation (or loanword) has maintained its popularity for over a century and a half, and has been transported into languages around the world. What remains a mystery to me is why many other short terms, such as SP for "small potatoes," NG for "no go," and BAE for "before anyone else," did not stand the test of time, and fell out of use. In the 1830s there were also teasing abbreviations like "SNAFU," believed to be of military origin, meaning "situation normal — all f...ed up." Clearly, this acronym suggested that all was *not* in order. Also, the short form OW for "oll wright" was among some of the ones that fell out of use. Historians tell us the OK abbreviation trend began in Boston and eventually spread throughout the western hemisphere, followed by the rest of the world. Others say that OK is of American-Indian origin, derived from the Choctow word okeh, which is used as a general affirmative, to indicate agreement.

Language is fascinating, and we all have a responsibility to use it consciously.

Every day, I'm reminded of a time when simplicity was more attainable than it is now. Each time, I'm made more aware of how, in this imperfect world, modern leadership, whether of a political or a corporate nature, seems to proceed without an instruction manual. Piloting from one quagmire to another, either at home or at work, requires time, patience and ingenuity. At times, when I'm confronted with a problem that threatens to rob my zeal, in order to avoid editorializing or making off-key gestures and comments, I try to step away from the situation, usually by heading outside for a breath of air. Sometime this works, other times it doesn't.

Peer-to-Peer support networks (and lunches gone awry)

One thing that helps is swapping stories with friendly peers. So, on a snowy Wednesday, my colleague, Jennifer, and I decided to take a break from our daily challenges and meet at a nearby restaurant for a quiet lunch. Our restaurant of choice that day was a small, rustic locale that offered a good buffet for a reasonable price, and enough space for eight square tables for four. Jennifer and I set out to enjoy a tender and juicy veal sandwich and a bottle of Perrier, and to share our knowledge and thoughts about goings on in our industry, our city, our province, the country and the wider world. Typically, we arrange lunch meetings in order to share recipes and talk about the traditions of foods and herbs that have been passed down to us from our predecessors. Sometimes we talk about music, upcoming events, books we're currently reading, or any other topic that happens to be of interest to us at that time.

On this day, the forty-five-minute interval away from the usual was meant to give us an opportunity to socialize and have a chance to talk about anything at all. We had no agenda, but perhaps we'd touch upon the day's events or have an opportunity to make light of an unpleasant situation from earlier in the day. It would also benefit us to break up our habit of eating alone at our desks, or wolfing down a sandwich while on the run to our next appointment.

Alas, our plan for a peaceful lunch date was scuttled by the group sitting two feet away from us. These lunch companions spoke so loudly that you'd think they were sitting at opposite ends of an airplane hangar. They shouted and laughed and hammed it up so much that it was impossible to ignore them, and they didn't seem to notice or care that they were making it impossible for us to hear each other or enjoy our meal. Boy, did they love to hear themselves talk! Looking at it from the other side of the coin, it's possible that they assumed the rest of the patrons were captivated by the unfolding drama. Everything that came out of their mouths said "I'm here and I'm the best." Their behaviour left us puzzled and wondering about their sense of themselves in relation to the rest of the world. What was it that compelled them to complain about every aspect of their lives, loudly, and in public? It was impossible not to overhear every word of their conversation, and their negativity was stunning. Their discontent covered every conceivable area of their lives, from their lousy work environments to the traffic on the roads, the high price of rent, and the nosy and intrusive habits of their in-laws. From this group, we learned that the weather sucked, that politicians were discombobulated, that the economy was a mess, and that the world in general was not a happy place. Nothing in life was simple or worthy of gratitude or praise. As we sat there, Jennifer and I could barely manage to say two words to each other; the high-decibel rants from the next table made us lose our train of thought.

It was obvious to us that these people thought their complaints were totally justified. Clearly, everyone else was to blame for their unhappiness. None of it was *their fault.* Trying to hide our puzzled looks, we bit our lips and secretly wondered what their employers must really think of their work performance. Were these four complainers even interested in trying to resolve any of their issues, or were they simply looking to be validated? Were these rebels looking to be rewarded in life without making any efforts to improve their lot?

We were tempted to slip them a note suggesting that they cool it with the complaining. We longed to be able to tell them to look for a way out of their unrealistic expectations and apparent unhappiness. Failing that, we were ready to recommend sedation. Their thinking did not seem to have any hope of moving beyond "me! me! me!" because *it wasn't their fault!* Life was really making things hard for them. My friend and I knew that it would only get harder if they didn't drop their selfish streak. At no point did any of these diners suggest that they bore even an ounce of personal responsibility for their unhappy lives. They seemed more interested in laying blame than in finding solutions. We didn't suppose any of them knew what John F. Kennedy meant when he wisely said: "Let us not seek to fix the blame for the past. Let us accept our own responsibility for the future." Maybe they never heard him speak at all.

Listening to these four ladies, it was hard to imagine that they would ever rise above their dejected state or abandon their blame-game. Jennifer and I had to stop ourselves from telling them that their disappointments may well be minimized if only they would try to accept responsibility for their own lives and happiness. Blaming others is a superficial tweak that feeds a temporary need for control, but it never really changes the fundamental message. Besides, these types of tweaks always come at a cost. Figuring that our input would be taken as nothing more than an insult, it was quite possible that our good intentions wouldn't have presented a cooperative solution. On that account, when in doubt, walk away!

Whispering to each other, Jennifer and I wondered if this group was on its last legs and was trying to stop the finger-pointing workout that had landed the blame for something that went wrong squarely on them. Maybe they were not happy to have a silent conversation in their head about what had led to a failed venture at the office on this day. If they could only see fit to refill their emotional cup with the painful truth, they might have to admit that when the project was assigned to them, the only thought circling their brain was: *"This is not my job."* Without a doubt, there's always more than one way to tell a story, but ultimately, it's how we tell it that matters. To us, their version seemed to lack a legitimate reason as to why the unacceptable outcome was due to someone else's shortfall. At this point, we couldn't help but speculate about what their supposedly nosy in-laws actually thought of their daughters-in-law. We could hardly imagine that the in-laws would consider these nitpickers to be a valuable addition to their families. We wondered if their in-laws were even interested in leaving an open door for compromise. Then again, were these folks even slightly interested in conciliation?

Complaining is not all bad. When used in the proper context, it can act as a natural venting system and can prevent undue stress and headaches. This is especially true if we have good friends or family members with whom we can share a burden. Expressing our dissatisfaction (as I am doing here) and sharing it with someone else can prove helpful if done with the purpose of achieving a more acceptable outcome. On the other hand, going overboard with complaints and being short on facts can potentially land us in a lot of hot water. Dishing out comments without sincerity and impartiality to substantiate the assertions is not the most effective way to find solutions either in our career or in our social circle. This is particularly true when we intend to support our claim for something the boss, a friend, or a relative, did wrong, which ultimately caused bitterness and resentment among the parties.

In business, rightly or wrongly, we've adopted a saying that the customer is always right. To me, this is a subject that takes on a different analysis. The road to right and wrong sits on the same bench as confidence and facts — and one person's certainty might be a threat to the other's confidence. Besides, if we allow the other to believe that facts don't matter in our personal life or at work, we're encouraging them to act like emotionless robots who can get rewarded for being a thorn in the side of everyone around them. I can attest to many occasions where my senior staff and I had to deal with frontline employees grumbling about their assignments and customers who took to complaining about the service they received, just to sound important or intellectually capable, or to show that they have creative intelligence. They like to give the impression they're "with it," and they cling to that illusion even when the evidence suggests otherwise.

Sometimes, I hypothesize that those who entertain bogus delusions find that waking up from restless nights is more wounding than admitting that the airs they put on during the day may not be a true reflection of who they are. People who are caught up in pretending to be someone they're not, can no longer distinguish between wisdom and foolishness. Maybe the reflection in their morning mirror can offer some assistance. If they're lucky, the manifestation may even be kind enough not to show misery in full outlines. Instead, it might display only bits and pieces of the frustration that engulfs them.

In the service industry, it's a known truth that an accumulation of repeated excuses for not meeting pre-set appointments, the inability to address issues at hand, insufficient product knowledge, or the boldness to let phone calls go unanswered, among other things, can all harm a company's reputation and undermine its ability to provide quality service. In like manner, hiding behind technical jargon in order to sound superior and highlight the other person's lack of technical lingo and knowledge is not the way to bring success to the company.

Likewise, people who hide behind feigned wisdom will often play the part of the victim and blame everyone around them for flattening their mood. Then, when they're unable to attract attention for their presumed competence, their mood sinks and the whining begins.

Whiners, for all intents and purpose, have personalized their policies and their narrow views of what they deem dreary and cannot zoom out to see the bigger picture. As such, they are like grown-ups who wouldn't be out of place in a kindergarten or a grade one class. To those of us who've had occasion to provide service to customers who tend to be a thorn in our side, I believe my tone will sound familiar.

From a business perspective, it's hard not to emphasize how their burdened attitude builds up the weight of carrying the "moron taxes" for corporations at large. When a company can afford to, it will hire professionals to be proactive and steer their enterprise away from that class of shallowness. Experience has taught me that, at times, when my company finds itself wedged in a situation that requires dealing with such employees or customers, it is best to pretend to go along with their self-serving biases and carry on as if nothing out of the ordinary has happened. So far, this has worked reasonably well, at least in the short-term. However, for long-term contracts, some type of corrective action has to be taken, or we'll be faced with a pitiable payoff and disappointing results.

All of this leads me to ask: *Are business and personal ethics under siege?*

It certainly felt like it during my recent business lunch with Jennifer. As if listening to the racket made by the four ladies sitting next to us was not enough to put us off our lunch, from the corner table we could also hear two distinguished-looking ladies replaying a recent night of debauchery. They were talking at high volume about all of the drinking and smoking they did with two rich men at a friend's house the previous night, and it was clear from their tone, the content of what they were saying, and their body language that both of them thought that this was perfectly acceptable behaviour. Did these ladies drink to be socially accepted, or because they were addicted to alcohol? Were they trying to mask their problems, or did they only want to experience what getting drunk felt like? What was their untold story?

On the surface, based on their appearance alone, these women presented an image of polished professionalism, or at least financial security. Their perfectly ironed clothes, blow-dried hair, expensive accessories and sharp-toed shoes combined to present an image of class, magnetism, and confidence. Their outer shell convincingly said that these ladies were serious about their appearance. They didn't just get up in the morning, get cleaned up, get dressed and go out; *they dressed to go out.* And in business, the way we dress usually tells a story about us and our personality. However, in this instance, it seemed clear that their clothes were telling a story that did not align with their inner selves. Were they being fanatics about fashion or were they communicating deceitful volumes about themselves? Maybe it was a little of both. Maybe it had something to do with the way they slept the night before.

Jennifer and I had no intention of eavesdropping, but the world is a stage, and curiosity won out. It may well be that these ladies wanted to test out the character of the gentleman sitting directly across from them — the one dressed in a slim-fitting charcoal wool suit, gray shirt and dark gray tie. The young man appeared to be spaced out and only vaguely aware of his surroundings. As the minutes ticked by, he gave no indication that he was focusing on anything, or that he was even remotely aware of his detachment. My colleague and I were unable to guess what was happening in his stupefied mind. He seemed to be so distracted that he didn't acknowledge anyone inside the restaurant. He was totally disconnected and looked like he was descending into a fog. What could have triggered that state of nothingness for this individual?

It was quite difficult to imagine making mental connections with the unconnected customers in this establishment today! Our take on the situation was that most of the patrons were not in a disheveled condition but only in an unhealthy state of mind. There was no shortage of chatting going on in the restaurant. We couldn't see how the situation would resolve itself or how we would be able to get the peaceful restaurant experience we were looking for. Why stick around any longer? Our weariness with complaints on one side and the pretentious posing on the other made it difficult to have any empathy for this crowd. Instead, their conversations made us feel trapped and anxious. We tried to trick ourselves into thinking that a few deep breaths could take the uneasiness away and allow us to carry on with our own conversation, but our anxiety kept rising and our spirits kept dropping.

Eventually, we agreed that our best option would be to pay the cheque and leave. So we did. A nice brisk walk seemed like just the thing to help clear our minds and lift our moods. As we turned the corner of the building, our attention was drawn to a city crew working to repair a watermain break at the end of the street. It was a bitterly cold day, and each of the workers standing above ground was holding a cup of coffee, which we presumed was meant to keep their hands warm and reduce the stress from the cold. As we got a little closer we could see that the men with the coffee cups were standing guard over a trench, making sure the workers below were safe and able to do their jobs. Inside the trench, two men were working to figure out how to weld the pipe without having to replace the sewer line.

We had no idea what kind of difficulties these men were facing, but it was striking to see how they braved the cold temperatures, which were made even more painful by the wind-chill index. They appeared calm and focused on their work, and didn't seem to mind having to wear multiple layers of loose clothing for better insulation, waterproof boots, and water-resistant gloves. Surely, we agreed, these men must have known when they signed up for the job that in the winter months, very cold weather increases the chances of pipe breaks. Obviously, that didn't deter them, because they took the job just the same. My friend and I took a few minutes to admire these workers, who suddenly began to look like artisans of the highest order. As we did, we realized that theirs was a different domain. They worked to repair whatever was broken in the city. They dealt with malfunctions of all kinds, regardless of the weather conditions. Their efforts benefitted the whole community, and made people physically comfortable, perhaps even ensured survival. What an achievement! These are the type of people who respond to real life needs, and who do so with solid dedication — sometimes even passion —instead of complaints.

Both of us developed a new appreciation that day for the contributions of trades people, and for their admirable dedication to their community. Until then, our opinion of the challenges these field workers faced during the cold winters and hot humid summers had been wrongly guided by our negative and unenlightened assumptions. In the past, we had underestimated their commitment to their work and the tangible benefits they brought to the whole community.

This observation, and the introspection it prompted in both of us, became the high point of our get-together. Jennifer and I agreed that our views and opinions of the people who work under such strenuous conditions had been opened to debate and correction. I wonder if we would have seen them in this new light without having just been surrounded by privileged whiners for the past hour. Certainly, the experience of listening to these people complain about their lives and their work made these men's contributions to the community stand out in stark contrast.

Back at my office, I needed a few minutes to process what I had just witnessed. Mostly, I was looking for a reasonable answer, or at least, a simple explanation regarding the origin of the human structure that makes us happy or wimpy, caring or impartial, loyal or false, conversant or oblivious to our surroundings. Not being one to look too far into scientific explanations, I turned to the social realm.

Society holds that every adult should be interested in getting an education, landing a good job, working their way through the ranks, being financially responsible, and standing ready to make a difference whenever possible. But not everyone is capable of achieving all of those things in equal measure. We all have different intellectual abilities, and not every conversationalist knows how to talk less and say more, or pay attention to what is being said. Viewpoints and skills differ from person to person. That variety is what makes society possible. It's our path to the future. Here, again, I'm referring to choices we make every day. Are we choosing wisely and positively so we can grow in wisdom, or are we opting to support negativity, manipulation, and abysmal behavior? Maybe we've developed our own win-win situation by pleading ignorance when it comes to dealing with risky and unpleasant things.

"I don't know"

Anywhere people engage in industry conversation as well as personal dealings, we're sure to hear the phrase "I don't know." Saying we don't know something might be the easiest way to skirt the truth or face having to make a decision. "I don't know" is a safety net. Making a decision means exposing oneself to the possibility of being right or wrong. By saying those three easy words, "I don't know," we let courage evade us and allow dignity to vanish; but it works! Once we utter those words, we probably feel as comfortable as if we're wearing an old pair of slippers. Every so often, we even use this phrase to keep our place in someone's good books. Other times, we simply utter it because we don't want people to say "I told you so" in the event we make a bad decision about something or someone. It could be that we say it because it's really difficult to be confident when we're asked to explain what might have possessed us to make such a blunder.

In my line of work, I hear the phrase "I don't know" at least fifty times a day, which, by my calculations, adds up to about 18,250 times a year. What I don't hear in the same capacity, though, is an explanation of the reason or circumstances that may have caused the person to make the blunder or omit passing specific details to the party in charge. Perhaps, a simple explanation such as the following one would go a long way: "I didn't have all the particulars of the assignment available, and in the interest of time, I had no choice but to move forward with the limited information at hand." Mistakes, when minimized, would not be so terrible, especially if the person involved, instead of jumping to the simplistic defense of "I didn't know," had taken the time to ask clarifying questions when the task was first assigned to them. It would also be refreshing to hear a simple "I'm sorry, I will use this experience to do better next time." There is nothing wrong with admitting to your supervisor that you were lacking the knowledge required to properly undertake that assignment. What can possibly be wrong with learning a new lesson from each experience? I don't think that giving a straightforward answer means that we're insensitive. The truth can sound offensive and at times it even sucks, but it does help us figure things out. And with that, we can walk toward autonomy sooner rather than later — like after we beat around the bush for a while.

Excuses and accountability

Have you ever been the recipient of self-justifying excuses from individuals who are never wrong or employees who bungle their days, pouting and complaining about a reprimand they deemed wrongly cast upon them by the supervisor? I have! In fact, I've experienced it many times, and each time, it took a bite out of my ability to listen.

Perhaps those who say "I don't know" frequently live within a naïve fantasy world in which they are sheltered from any accountability. Yes, accountability. Here we go again with that tricky word. Isn't accountability the most frustrating concept? As far as I can tell, accountability is not a one-time thing; it's such an insatiable pledge that it doesn't shy away from demanding ongoing commitments from us. And, when we try to skirt it for any reason, we are diminished. Being accountable for everything we say and do means taking ownership of our actions. When things go awry, by taking our actions seriously, we'll step into the "figure out a solution mode" in order to fix what failed. In business, by avoiding accountability, we fall back into that uninspiring, self-fulfilling mode which most of the time is a last-ditch attempt at avoiding the feedback that says "I told you this would happen."

Grab the reins!

Whether accountability works for most people or only a small percentage of us, in my experience, it stands as the major factor distinguishing between success and forfeiture. If the past years have taught me anything about life's rollercoaster of emotions, unending responsibilities at work and at home, the struggle to achieve a goal, the value of a social circle, and taking responsibility for my own actions, it's that if you place yourself at the bottom of the human scale, you will, and not without logical basis, have the feeling that everything around you is miserable and worthless. And when that state of affairs takes hold, nothing will ever improve. Looking back, I fully understand the reasons why working hard and staying unwavering in our efforts to achieve our purpose in life will lessen the distance to satisfaction. If you aspire to be on the right side of the divide, do not let yourself fall into a lackluster state.

Instead, get out of that trap and accept accountability. Get it?

As Roy T. Bennet, author and thought leader, said, "Make improvements, not excuses. Seek respect, not attention."

To win the struggle, it is important to ditch the constant excuses that are nothing but a cover-up for a deceitful story, an illusion of our present being, a short-cut to nowhere, and a meaningless way of engaging with the world. Denial can be a complex nest. The truth is much simpler to manage; it can quiet our distress, soften animosity, promote loyalty, allow us to let go of unwanted baggage and, simplify our lives.

CHAPTER 6

CHAPTER 6

ACTUALITIES

From time to time, my colleagues and I get together to enjoy a coffee and compare notes about our business and personal lives. We do this to remind ourselves that we are not alone and to brainstorm solutions to common issues and problems. Once we get talking, the words rush out so quickly that you would think we hadn't spoken to another human being in a month. When our conversations touch upon the value of truth and honesty, our thoughts begin to connect like lightning reaching from the clouds to the ground.

More than once, we've expressed concern that truth telling and civility may be going out of style. We also worry about a decline in people's willingness to seek out ways to compromise with others in their daily business and personal lives. As a society, it sometimes feels like we may be on a collision course between proven operating practices and the tendency for people to simply shrug their shoulders and say *"not my problem."* Have you ever experienced the challenge of ordering a coffee in a shop where you almost have to speak the coffee lingo before the order is processed? But, that's not the barista's fault!

Things really are different today than they were one or even two decades ago. For instance, today, most of us chat on video, network on social media, and pay for that complicated cup of coffee with the tap of a debit card to an ATM terminal — no pin required. We use a tablet to check the weather forecast and news updates, and we rely on the Pillboxie app to remember to take our meds. And yet not everyone has joined the technical revolution. All of these conveniences represent a complicated way of doing things for those who are afraid to press a button on the keyboard for fear of breaking the computer. We can't simply shrug our shoulders at their dismay or say "get over it" if we have no insight into their apprehensions for experimenting with new technology.

Also on this list of new ways of doing things is the challenging task of finding companionship. We're all prone to feeling lonely from time to time, and searching for companionship is no easy task. The process went from the organic way of meeting someone to simply affixing a check mark in the comradeship box. This may very well work for the younger generation, but for older adults, online dating can be outright alienating.

How do we reconcile these positions to make this new method equally acceptable to both generations? Could we look to the adult education system to re-work their structure to include classes or seminars on how best to help seniors find a way to beat isolation? Might that be the missing ingredient that could create an ambiance of confidence followed by a good reputation? I think so, and I would venture to add that anything that improves our social status is good for our community in a larger sense.

Such restructuring might even help us develop a stronger democratic system and a more promising future marked by stronger connections between customer and supplier, parents and offspring, teachers and students, management and employees, preachers and parishioners.

I like to believe that people prefer to deal with certainty instead of ambiguity. Furthermore, in the event things don't quite pan out to our liking, we can find solace in Mark Twain's quote: "For every problem, there is a solution that is simple, neat — and wrong." Although this may be a bit of a stretch, trying to solve a problem can often be an enjoyable and rewarding experience. Facing the possibility that some activities will not yield positive results, experience will, nonetheless, reward those individuals who possess the desire and prudence to address each crisis. This practice can be deemed an essential part of most jobs. What's more, it's not limited to the service industry, police officers, private investigators, teachers or entrepreneurs. We can all be problem solvers to some degree or another, even if we don't always hit our target. Some of us may excel in solving 'people problems,' whereas others are good at diagnosing operational issues or working-out logical solutions to cognitive challenges. Try solving a problem; see what happens when you're willing to put in the effort and take a chance on your capabilities!

Mentoring for success

In the business world, one encounters entrepreneurs who like to go it alone, fix only what is broken, and build something prestigious from the bottom up. While a business leader may have good intentions and exciting ideas, those strengths can be enhanced further by adding a mentor to the mix. Mentors can offer essential guidance on how to build a sustainable operation. I've lived through days when I was just about ready to let business challenges break me, and, at the time, I might have given up, if not for my mentor telling me I could work through whatever landed on my desk. Of course, mentoring is not to be confused with therapy, and mentoring itself is not a magical skill. A mentor's desire to help others can only be effective if the mentee has an open attitude, is capable of learning, and is willing to take responsibility for making things happen. It takes effort, a stellar configuration, and most of all, the willingness to share good experiences as well as bad ones. With an open mind and a sincere readiness to deepen my knowledge, I practiced putting my worries on hold and focused on winning strategies instead. Had I not paid attention to the case examples and the candid insight shared by my mentor, my life might have turned out very differently. And I believe almost any business person could benefit from working with a mentor. We all have room to grow and a role to play in life's game, so why not buy into that plan?

On a typical day, I believe most of us get very concerned with "what if" situations — so much so that this type of thinking becomes a part of our everyday life. But when we indulge in thinking about what ifs too often, it can cause a drain on our emotional strength, our personal life, and our business dealings. It's dangerous to spend too much time ruminating about worst case scenarios. It's much better to focus on what is right in front of us, and search for ways to get ahead of the query. From there we can better observe how to turn things around to our best interest.

One problem a lot of security companies face, especially the physical (guard) security providers, is that we all seem to be cut from the same cloth when it comes to the tendency to worry. We wouldn't be in the security industry in the first place if we weren't already naturally cautious people. So, when I'm faced with worrisome questions, such as: will the guard show up on time at their assigned post, will they arrive in full uniform, will they follow proper protocol, will they be vigilant and stay safe, I put my own anxiety aside and urge the supervising staff not to overreact if they encounter such issues. By modeling calm behaviour, I help to ensure that my supervisors are able to remain calm and do their best to deal with any given situation in a diplomatic and firm manner. Even though I give myself permission to put my worry aside in these moments, this does not mean that it's forgotten or cleared from my mind. The worry is merely pushed into a new compartment, labeled "to be dealt with later." In actuality, the issue doesn't leave my space until I can address it with a less clouded mind, after the worry has had a chance to lose steam. There is always the likelihood that problems, big or small, are solvable. The best course of action is to evaluate the options available and move forward with a clear and concise plan of action. For the most part, I find that a solid game plan is an up-to-snuff calculus capable of reducing worry and stress.

Collegial relationships can be incredibly rewarding. When Jennifer (my lunch companion in the last chapter) and I first decided to meet for coffee, it was just a small gesture that included a ten-minute exchange and a handshake. But we agreed to keep meeting on a regular basis so we could swap stories, learn from each other, and help each other assess the pros and cons of action or inaction on any given issue. This course of action may sound a little surprising to some, but for us, the creative positivity that we derive from these coffee meetings has been a blessing throughout our careers.

Today, we refer to our coffee shop meetings as the hub of resolution time. And I'll say this: the longer you've been in the workforce or in a leadership role, the greater the odds that the suggestion of a coffee meeting will sound like a pretty good idea. You don't need to worry about formalities; no one is judging you, and you don't have to dive into business talk right away. For us, an invitation to a coffee meeting has become something that's very hard to turn down. We both look forward to the kick of an espresso or a cappuccino as we evaluate our current work or personal situations and consider different perspectives without having to be official. In the unlikely possibility that we have nothing new to talk about on the work front, we turn our attention to other topics. Hope and helplessness, the economy, rules and disobedience, laws and obstruction of justice, honesty and affliction, and worry and assurance are some of the other subjects that keep us involved. We both appreciate open discourse as it is what makes the whole thing meaningful for us.

A recurring topic of interest for both of us has to do with the utility or futility of 'worry.' Yes, I'm sure we all know what it feels like to worry, and I'm equally convinced that none of us likes it.

But, according to some experts, worry can act as an emotional buffer, and the right amount of it is actually good for us. In our everyday being, worrying can motivate us to not only have plan "A" in place, but also have plan "B" standing by, if only for purposes of being able to worry less about unforeseen circumstances. Worrying helps us to be more prepared, and preparation helps to alleviate worry. It can be a beneficial cycle. The real deal here is to know just how much worry is enough, without tipping over into anxiety.

Both Jennifer and I know people who worry "too little" (which is to say, they almost never worry about anything, leaving that to others) and others who worry to excess, about everything. As such, we tend to get excited about sharing stories of people who occupy both ends of the spectrum (the spectrum of different worrying types, that is), and others who seem to have found a workable balance. We agree that non-worriers seem to fool themselves into thinking that unpleasant things will not happen to them. They seem to think that if they simply float through life, they will continue to enjoy good luck. But that doesn't always work out, and the non-worriers have a tendency to be unprepared when bad things happen. The over-worriers, meanwhile, get to feeling so tense that they can't think clearly. Their brain becomes frozen, and they are unable to process information or take action. Silly things such as being seen picking your nose, momentarily forgetting your phone number, being heard making a noise while doing your business in the washroom, having a bit of spit squirt out of your mouth while you're talking to someone, or addressing a person by the wrong name, are all things that shouldn't qualify as long-term worries because no one will remember them after a few days, or at most weeks. And yet a person who worries too much often gives such trivialities much more importance than they deserve. It can be helpful to remember that no one cares about you being "perfect" as much as you care about yourself, and therefore any small misstep or embarrassment is likely to be forgotten by others almost as soon as it happens.

Over 500 years ago, Michel de Montaigne, one of the most significant philosophers of the French Revolution, made the following statement: "My life has been filled with terrible misfortunes, most of which never happened." And modern research bears out this thought. Studies have shown us that about 85 percent of what we worry about never happens and, the 15 percent that does happen is usually something we can deal with and learn from.

When worry becomes anxiety

The tendency to worry too much is often known as catastrophizing. An example of someone who lives his days predicting calamities is my long-time friend James. His mind has been paralyzed by worry and fear for many years. This territorial predator has dominated his psyche in such a manner that worry and fear often cause him to experience anxiety and physical illness. Paranoia also plays a role. He senses intimidation attempts where none exist, and he tends to see anything that happens as an attempted put-down of his persona. His worry-induced state prevents him from keeping a job, nurturing friendships, focusing on the facts before him, and understanding the reality that is being proposed to him. In this man's world, worry is a formidable enemy that has had a serious impact on his quality of life.

For those of us who worry less and take action more, I believe it's true that we tend to look at problems for what they really are and then forge ahead with the action we feel is most sensible. By not letting worry bog us down, we're able to look at a production flaw or a personal matter as a 'bug' or a 'blip' rather than a common occurrence. In my industry, a big part of the service staff's daily responsibilities is to deal with glitches and blips of the electronic equipment that can at times disable the functionality of a security system. For these technicians, worrying about the same thing over and over again is an unproductive use of time. For the most part, they come to work each day with renewed resolve to figure out a solution that best addresses the issues facing them, and at the end of the day, they go home with a sense of satisfaction.

I have no doubt there are tangible benefits to be gained by remaining realistic and taking pragmatic steps to live a life of fewer worries. Such a life is calmer and tends to correspond with higher satisfaction levels and better health. Staying moored to reality (as opposed to ruminating on things that *might* happen or *might* be true) also teaches us to focus on what is in front of us. This can help tackle the tendency to be scattered or to allow ourselves to be overwhelmed by neurotic thoughts and desires. By keeping things authentic and undemanding, we can shift our focus away from unpleasant happenings that may or may not come our way and pay more attention to the tangible steps we need to take in order to have a good life.

My colleague and I are also interested in the way some people complain rather than to take action. We have explored this tendency over the course of many coffee meetings, trying to get at the root of this behaviour. We have entertained a wide range of possibilities for why people grumble without taking steps to change their circumstances. Some people may get into a loop of complaining without acting because they're bored on the job, or unhappy with their looks, or because they want to escape from their current problem. Others, we surmise, may find it hard to deal with things in a mature way because they were emotionally arrested in childhood by a trauma or a negative family experience. Others may be genetically incapable of redirecting their negative thoughts or turning thought into action. Still others may be starved for attention, and just want to feel valued and noticed. There are many possible reasons for this type of approach to life, and doubtless as many solutions as there are causes.

A few years back, our company employed a middle-aged man whose behaviour shook us to the core. Almost immediately after he joined our group, he pleaded to be allowed to work as many overtime hours as possible, saying he needed it to be able to afford food and lodging. His account of surviving hard times and narrowly dodging the ultimate call in his home country convinced us to make a gut-based decision and forgo the usual protocols for deciding such cases. Out of sympathy for his situation, we overlooked the pros and cons and ignored the extra costs to our company of allowing him as much overtime as he was requesting. Gut decisions usually reflect our feelings, and in this case, we felt we were helping a man desperately trying to get back on his feet.

Within weeks, cracks began to appear in his story and in his persona. It became apparent that he had an unyielding need to be noticed and prized. Added to that was his intense craving to be recognized as the 'one and only' top employee of the month each and every month. He freely shared his life stories of dangerous adventures, speaking of adrenaline triggers, and recounting his difficult escapes from danger as if to re-test his will and spirit. We were in awe of his nerve, strength, and determination to survive as he trekked the road to personal mending. At first, we wondered how this man managed to separate all that hurt and despair from his past and redefine himself by pushing ahead at whatever cost. But in time we came to believe that he was a fraud, and that his past tribulations may have been of his own making.

It's possible that he did actually suffer some trauma. Maybe, he couldn't compartmentalize his despair anymore because it had already affected most aspects of his life. If only we could have seen this act in a clearer light during the interview, we may have been able to untangle those twisted wires and said "no thanks" before the meeting was over. But, as it turned out, in the face of his finely detailed information, we unquestioningly accepted his uncorroborated stories of past bravery and even admired his boldness. We fell especially hard when he told us about his cruel encounter with the outlaws who carried out the kidnapping of his brother's six-year-old son. Notably, that episode came with two different endings; one spoke of the young boy eventually being returned safely to his family due to his fearless heroism, and the other had a sourer closing. He loved every second of attention he was drawing from management staff, his co-workers and customers alike.

In time, his chronicle began raising a few eyebrows. This man was a pro at embellishing his stories and making them a hit. Once, he even went as far as having a box of food delivered to our office, claiming he was sharing a gift he had received from a secretive charitable organization. The origin of the gift box was somewhat suspicious. We had never heard of a charitable organization operating in secret. Worse, the awkwardness of the quantity of items contained in the package made it difficult to conceal our confusion without violating the social gift-receiving norm. Noticing our apprehension, he became unquestionably perplexed. As we watched his demeanor start to crumble, we saw him quickly regain his composure and start playing the afflicted card.

Unfortunately, our company's budget did not allow for a psychologist on the payroll, so we had to rely on our own instincts to distinguish what was fake in his story from what was real. Weeks later, we finally saw through his act and cut ties with him — and not without a cost to the company. We had been duped! For a while, we had mistakenly believed he was real when he was not. Because we had erred on the side of laxity, we got scammed. Even though our human resources team prides itself on being natural skeptics, we still fell for this man's deception.

Lessons learned

As much as we tried to be supportive of each other, we couldn't help but feel upset and embarrassed that we had allowed a fraudster infiltrate our ranks and beat us to the money drawer. Although we had paid out many unnecessary overtime hours, we learned that these types of people are so good at what they do that even someone with a vivid imagination can fall victim to their ploy. Consequently, these kinds of encounters often push employers to be super vigilant, and to avoid extending trust to potential employees, even when they might want to. Such encounters can cause owners to suspend some of the openness that they might otherwise have liked to apply to their business practice.

For a person in charge, these occurrences touch upon their philosophical dimension in the same way the loss of a puppy makes people weep and ache. In our personal space, we like to say that we learn by trial and error, and believe it or not, that holds true for corporations as well.

Businesses need to make mistakes in order to accelerate their competitiveness. That being so, the fact remains that profits and rewards are typically gauged by the company's success and not by how well we manage to learn our lessons as we go along. Trials and miscalculations can have recognizable value, if only to encourage business owners to give a new idea a try. Be that as it may, we should not move forward with an unknown or unproven idea or employee until we've done our proper investigation and are confident that the scheme, or the person, will work to our advantage. In the event the outcome does not meet our anticipated expectations, the cost of the trial should come with a minimal price tag attached to it. The walk-away lesson ought to add value and creativity to our marketing plans.

CHAPTER 7

CHAPTER 7

MOTIVATING EXCUSES

Purposely forgetting things and deliberately not remembering to complete assigned tasks can be an excellent defense mechanism and a good way to shake blame off our shoulders. That's if anyone believes in our justification.

As children and teens, we all took for granted that our parents would be easily deceived when we said we *"forgot"* to do our chores, or our math assignment, or that the history project was due already, or that we had to clean our room. Surely, that was not always the case. Most likely, our parents were not deceived by our creative performance at all. They merely wanted to give us a pass on that day. What we didn't detect at the time is that they kept mental notes on the rate of recurrence of our pranks. As far as school was concerned, we did not grasp or share in the knowledge that parents had two things going for them: the teacher would call them to keep them abreast of any situation that needed attention, and the report card would paint a clear picture of our learning progress and habits.

As we grew up and gained a better understanding of how the world worked, we figured out that the excuse of having forgotten something only worked a small percentage of the time. Our parents had us all figured out. For instance, we didn't forget that they promised to buy us new clothes or a new bike, to paint our room, to increase our weekly allowance, to let us stay up later on Friday nights, or to let our friends sleep over anytime we asked. Anything fun was firmly lodged in our memories, while drudgery like homework and house chores were sporadically thrown on the chopping block.

There is a very fine line between keeping a selective memory and not telling the truth. Almost all teenagers have, at one time or another, purposely not disclosed all facts to their parents, especially when they were asked about who they associated with and whether they were drinking or participating in any other bad habits. If someone was to tell me that they never lied as a teenager, I'd say they lied then and they're lying right now.

The unfortunate thing about lying is that after you've been discovered a few times you lose people's trust, and when you actually tell the truth, no one will believe you. And teens are not the only ones who do it. Far from it, in fact. Adults are quite adept at spinning or massaging the truth, particularly when it comes to dishing out fake flattery. Smooth talking might get a passing mark if the message is delivered for the purpose of protecting someone's feelings or boosting their morale. It may also work out well when the result is going to be better than if told the whole truth. In this case, I'm of the opinion that making a person feel good should be considered more valuable than keeping the compliment unadulterated. For instance, telling a bride that she looks stunning is much better than saying, "Wow, your makeup is of ultra-fine quality!" The same applies if you meet someone for lunch and you're aware they're totally broke, but they lie and offer to pay the bill. Do you make them sweat it out or do you say: "Oh no, this one is on me, I insist!" I think you'll agree with me that empathy is worth an awful lot to most of us, and dispensing it is not so hard to do. What's more, it helps us normalize our own emotions so we can understand what it feels like to walk in the other person's shoes.

We don't have to be in denial to believe that delivering a puffed-up comment with a pinch of honesty and a little softness may well mean that telling a white lie is the least offensive alternative. Every so often, we tend to stretch the truth when we get caught breaking a rule. This holds especially true when we're caught driving over the speed limit. I wouldn't want to count the number of times police officers hear a falsehood when they stop speeding vehicles and ask the drivers if they're aware they were hitting eighty-two in a sixty-mile zone. The answers are pretty much one and the same: "Sorry officer, but I'm sure I was doing only sixty-two miles per hour." The fact is this white lie seldom absolves us of our responsibility to obey the road signs— in the name of safety.

Let's not forget about the multicoloured lie that is often told to avoid marital punishment — if the lie even succeeds. Here is a story of a former employee who had a habit of telling his partner the reason he got home late and didn't call to advise he'd be working a few extra hours was because the phone system at the office was temporarily disabled and the cell phone battery was drained. Meanwhile, his battery was being recharged with another partner at an undisclosed location.

Today, as working adults of the world, we continue to make excuses for our actions, whether we need to or not. When the truth is inconvenient, we enlarge the fibre of the story enough so we can reel-off the same old *"I forgot"* or *"it just slipped my mind"* excuse as a mindful coping strategy. To that, we've also added the *"I thought the other person was taking care of it"* contour when we don't fancy working on a particular task. The same strategy comes into play when we choose to let something slide, hoping it won't surface again because we're intimidated by the size of the project or because we didn't intent to work on it at all. By pulling out this excuse, we tend to feel we have protected our self-image. Using a certain amount of dishonesty and self-deception may not bring about any serious consequences; however, it may not conform to our personal narrative either.

If you're like me, a seasoned collector of these excuses, I'll bet you've devised an official anti-excuse escape plan by now. I'm referring to a plan that leads the way for people who suffer from a faltering memory to come up with better-quality made-up facts when they find themselves under pressure. At minimum, they should offer a bit more detail to back up their stories. A little insight into the difficulties they encountered will give their tale a degree of credence and might even be more readily accepted.

I learned fairly early on in my career that throwing a fit when you catch an employee in a phony excuse is not a well-played reaction. At times, though, an unedited venting can be quite healthy. By the same token, going off on a rant when a friend or family member tells us they didn't have a free minute to answer our call or respond to our email is not the best way to conduct ourselves. Although, we're well aware that they probably just didn't want to connect with us, it's still wise not to let on that we've been offended by their inaction. An old-fashioned rant may make us feel better in that moment, but it will make it difficult to be around those same people at the next gathering. At the end of it all, lying remains a universal feature of our everyday life.

Pareto's Principle

Vilfredo Federico Damaso Pareto, an esteemed civil engineer, economist, sociologist and political theorist of Italian origin (1848–1923), introduced us to the 20/80 decision-making rule, which is also known as Pareto's Principle. This principle referred to his observation that eighty percent of Italy's wealth was owned by twenty percent of the population. When it comes to telling the truth, statistically, Pareto's observation asserts that twenty percent of the people tell eighty percent of the lies, and eighty percent of the people account for the remaining twenty percent of the lies. Surely, we've all come across people who make a deliberate attempt to distort the truth in an effort to gain attention, or simply because they get a kick out of lying.

In business, we think of the 80/20 rule as a simple case of cause and effect — 80 percent of the company's revenue is generated by 20 percent of its customers. This rule can be used to identify the inputs that could potentially be the most productive and make them a preference. Although this observation is a precept and not a precise percentage, it's nevertheless a helpful tool when planning for future endeavors. In more general terms, most things in life are not distributed evenly. However, Pareto's Principle helps us realize that the majority of gains come from the minority of inputs, for example:

- 20 percent of the employees contribute 80 percent of the results
- 20 percent of the wardrobe is used 80 percent of the time
- 80 percent of the absenteeism is due to 20 percent of the employees
- 80 percent of the consequences come from 20 percent of the causes

I know I share this notion with many other members of our industry when I say that nowadays, it's not uncommon to be dealing with employees who believe they are very masterful at delivering self-preserving excuses. I'm of the opinion that these people would be hard-pressed to pull out all the stops in the hope of changing their game when their conduct is called into question. Nothing anyone might say to them would boost their daily output, let alone their sense of duty or their personal capabilities. I have come to accept that I do have a role to play in helping to shore up their much-needed self-esteem, weak excuses, or poor decision-making ability, as long as doing so doesn't get in the way of my making the most of every working hour.

Finally, *and I mean finally,* I've come to the conclusion that action and inaction can be considered companions, of a sort, even though they differ completely. One (action) pushes performance, while the other (inaction) foreshadows the deed by stifling performance. We could probably make quite a convincing argument as to the reason we choose one or the other, as long as we can come up with a persuasive answer to the why and why-not questions that follow. And that is something that can be painful to attempt. Concocting motivating excuses may come easily for some people, but it can be awfully stressful for others. Either way, to be successful with a discourse, the person delivering the speech should be judged on two levels: firstly, did the given response achieve the objective, and secondly, did it convince the other person to connect with the speaker's train of thoughts. On the first level, where action is in question, it usually fails because no objective is accomplished. On the second level, there is a pretty good chance the mission is abortive; no display of persuasion will be manifested on the receiving party's face.

Inaction, although a safe bet and a preferred choice for many people, can turn out to be our enemy and a demolisher of human and business potential. In contrast, it's no secret that action leads to small bouts of hurried change. It must, therefore, be a good idea to allow room for small wins so they can pave the way for larger milestones. Given that it is highly unlikely that anyone will achieve perfection, in today's business world, lateral thinking is of the essence. A can-do attitude is the most effective way to speak up for action.

There is one other element of inaction that yanks me out of my business perspective; the violation of a clean and orderly office norm. More than ever, this involves the food galley, or the place where employees eat. I'm touching upon those who appear to suffer from sanitation impairment, not to mention the ones who are oblivious to the responsibility of removing their dirty mugs and cleaning their messy desks. Incentivizing these people to be tidier by offering food or coffee coupons does not always motivate them toward cleanliness. Let me tell you, similar to many other people in the workforce, I've been through a few dreadful encounters where I stepped too close to someone's desk and the odour from the putrefied food hiding in their drawer attacked my nostrils. Even after I pinched my nose shut, I experienced moments of social anxiety because anything I might say about the offensive smell could hurt or humiliate the other person. My key point here is that the physical environment of our work station has a profound effect on the way we conduct ourselves. By not keeping our thumb on the company's philosophical pulse in addition to keeping our work station in disarray and emitting putrid fumes, we portray the image of a muddled operator. This trademark is especially unsympathetic where hotdesking (sharing desk space with others) is in practice. The new trend of desk-sharing is meant to improve the company's efficient use of desks and chairs. By having employees share desk space, the employer reduces operational space, office furniture, and hardware costs. The concept is based on the idea that in a typical environment, approximately thirty to forty percent of office furniture remains unused most of the time due to people being on vacation, out on errands, or away sick. But, not everyone is in favour of this flexible arrangement. There are a number of reasons for that, and public health is definitely a major distress point. Even by getting buy-in from the employees and making this type of arrangement an ongoing forum, there is no assurance that hygiene etiquette will be upheld. Hotdesking is an easy way to pass germs from one person to another, especially when people share phone and office supplies. Other factors that pinch the employees' forbearance for this arrangement is having to adjust the height of the chair each time they use it, clean someone else's crumbs off the desk, and at times, having to dispose of the previous employees' dirty Kleenex because *they forgot* to do so prior to leaving the spot.

I get the distinct feeling that desk-sharing isn't as seamless a transition from the norm as some employers would like it to be. True, the old ways are mutating into the new, but believe it or not, even the millennial, who as we know, are the first generation to grow up with shared space and smart technology and, who appear to like moving as frequently as work asks them to, experience some anxiety with this system. I have to question if hotdesking provides us with any mitigation room for personal identity space. I'm referring to available desk space for things such as family pictures, achievement awards, personal calendars or any trinket that speaks of us in the first person. I don't know what the acceptable answer is, or how much it matters to most people. In the meantime, it seems to me that the main issue with desk-sharing remains one of cleanliness. From my perspective, the person who leaves a messy desk due to poor habits sends an adverse message about personal ethics and may suffer consequences when it comes to career advancement. So, take action, turn it around, and keep your desk clean.

CHAPTER 8

CHAPTER 8

BLUNDERS AND BLUNDERERS

Growing up brings new adventures. From the beginning, adults encourage children to learn life's ropes, become self-sufficient, achieve good grades at school, and master social skills. As children get older, they soak up life's knowledge and their priorities start to change. Many young people make their way to college and university, hoping to graduate with honours. For others, getting through high school is a hassle, and a college or university education is beyond their reach.

Wherever they are headed, every young person has to transition from the playfulness of being a child to the responsibilities of becoming an adult. Embracing this transition may be difficult for the type of person who shies away from imagination or feels slighted when they discover that their dreams may not really matter much to anyone else. Once they begin to see the new path stretching ahead of them, they face the challenge of landing a good job and moving out on their own. If mother luck sees fit to extend them a financial opening to purchase a used vehicle, they've made great strides toward personal autonomy. Then, as adults in charge of their own destiny, they feel the need for a little entertainment money and the potential to stretch their income far enough to include buying pre-cooked meals or fresh groceries for the purpose of preparing superb healthy dinners, and all other essential needs. Let's not leave out a membership to a fitness club, as physical exercise is celebrated as the route to good health (both mental and physical) and longevity. Of course, the daily agenda also includes paying the bills, acquiring the latest electronic devices for speedy communication, and everything else in between.

Now, in the midst of all this, a person is bound to make a few mistakes as well as several blunders. We might think that there is no difference between a blunder and a mistake, but I submit that there is. When we're careless or clumsy, we're prone to make blunders. Let's just say that if we're quick to blurt out something about a situation we know nothing about, there's a pretty good chance we'll muck it up and blunder our way through it. But, when we take inappropriate action, whether on purposes or by using bad judgment, we'll most definitely make mistakes. The good thing is that no one is perfect. We're all susceptible to both blunders and mistakes. The important thing is that we have an opportunity to learn from such experiences and do a better job the next time a similar situation comes up. If we can do that, we don't need to jump to the wrong conclusion about the value of our personality traits.

Is a blunder less wicked than a mistake? Perhaps. It all depends on the size of the misstep, the degree of intentionality at work, and the cost, or the consequences. I'd like to share a story that was told by one of my business acquaintances not long before the writing of this book. He was made aware of a big mistake one of his employees made while servicing a longstanding customer's machinery needs. As I listened to each and every word he said about the incident, all I could do was flop down in my chair in disbelief. By the time I had heard the full story, I understood his concern and his trepidation about possibly losing the account. His employee had totally lost his composure when the customer asked him to address a second issue after he finished repairing the main item of concern. This serviceman was so engrossed in solving the first problem that being asked to do something else made him light up like a match, and he actually told the customer to "F--k off and don't bother me — I'm busy." To make matters worse, he did not follow up with an apology for his outburst, nor did he have any intention of assuming responsibility for his behaviour.

I think I was struck more by my acquaintance's description of the serviceman's demeanor than by the magnitude of the mistake. With his selection of eight unwarranted words, this man managed to create an embarrassing and awkward situation that would be hard to remedy. This employee had tripped the wrong switch. My associate's response to this stressful situation was to boil over like a tea kettle. At one point during his venting session I suggested he go for a jog around the block in order to blow off more steam. Since this was not a do-or-die situation, he needed to figure out how best to correct the error and soothe the client's bruised sensibilities. He also needed to know how to deal with his employee. But, figuring out why people make such dim-witted mistakes is very difficult. A situation like this is much more damaging to a company than sending out an unedited email, making an ugly face, giving someone the finger, or brushing off someone's distress. In business, as in everyday life, these occurrences cannot be explained away with the philosophy that "we're always in a rush and don't have time to think things through properly." A situation like this runs deeper than that, and may speak to an impulse-control problem that needs to be addressed before an employee can be trusted again. That's if they can be trusted to represent the company at all.

The reality is that we can make our day-to-day operations and processes a little less stressful with tiny adjustments here and there. We can learn to showcase non-creepy smiles in order to pass positive vibes to our customers, and we can practice getting more sleep at night to avoid foggy thinking the next day. To those suggestions we can reinforce habits like taking time to proofread emails before pressing the 'send' key, editing memos before circulating them to the office staff, and re-thinking what we really want to say, or should be saying, to a boss or a friend. It may seem like a never-ending burden, but we cannot go wrong by revisiting and improving our communication skills. Better to spend a few moments looking something over one last time than to risk having to beat ourselves up when judgmental readers catch our mistakes.

Today, we're living in a world where many things are competing for our attention at the same time. So far, I have yet to find a productivity hack that can help us shorten that list. Many people hold to the conformist idea that keeping busy is the way to thrive in today's fast-paced world. But, quite often, busyness gets out of control, in most cases it happens at a time when deadlines are impossible to meet. Without a magic formula to address the overflow, it's easy to make an unconscious mistake. In fact, it's our fast-paced work world, where everyone is expected to be busy all the time that creates the conditions for blunders and mistakes that are serious enough to require more than a simple email to set the record straight.

All of this applies as much to yours truly as to anyone. I candidly admit that on more than one occasion I've processed incorrect computer entries, misspelled an addressee's name, or written an inaccurate date on a document— to name only a few of my inadvertent blunders over the years. But, I take comfort in the fact that I'm hardly alone. As proof (if any were needed), I offer the following examples of written notices that some busy individuals posted without the benefit of proofreading:

A memo circulated among the field staff reminding them to sanitize their hands before leaving a site.

Please wash your hands before *living* the site.

A no-parking note attached to the overhead door of a cement factory.

> Staff parking only.
> Illegally parked vehicles will be ***fine*** and towed at owner's expense.

An in-patient parking notice posted at the rear of a walk-in clinic.

> ***Impatient*** parking only

An acknowledgement note sent by a title agent to the insurance company with regards to the defalcation clause (a form of embezzlement clause). The agent accidentally wrote: defecation clause (bowel movement)

> I read and understood the ***defecation*** clause as stated in this agreement.

Although these errors likely did no more than put a smile on the faces of the people who noticed them, a little editing would have clarified the messages and prevented possible embarrassment.

Other blunders are more serious. Some common ones involve things like complaining to a co-worker about your boss's poor attitude, or about the workload that's being dumped on you. These can be tough situations to get out of if your venting is not kept confidential.

Unfortunately, a simple apology is not always enough to recover from this kind of mishap. As we advance far enough in our career and reach a position of authority, it's advantageous to take note of our predecessors' experiences, as they, too, learned about the perils of gossiping, speaking out of turn, or divulging operational or personal details on the job. The problem with saying too much is that it tends to alienate people who may feel uncomfortable with the information you so freely imparted. Our colleagues' misadventures can teach us that it's not in our best interest to disclose too many disconcerting business particulars to a work associate, regardless of whether we consider them to be trustworthy or not. Instead, it's a lot wiser to speak about work-related stresses to our life partner, who may be in a better position to hear us out and perhaps soothe our frustration with a glass of wine or a bowl of ice cream —whatever hits the mark. Another smart choice that I think works very well is to talk to a pet. As silly as this may sound, we can at least be sure that the pet won't let out a peep. But, if we choose to voice our anxiety to co-workers, then it's safe to assume that our concerns *will* get out sooner or later, and not in the manner we expressed them. Then again, if you're looking for a payoff, by all means, gossip away; under those circumstances, you don't care if your words are passed onto your employer because if they opt to release you from the company, they have to offer a severance package.

One specific blunder that unnerves me has to do with employees who freely leave copies of their employment applications on their desk while they hunt for another job. Even in a workplace where tolerance levels are generally high, this kind of thing is out of bounds.

Technology has made it easy for people to look for work, and disloyal employees have been known to do their online career searches while on the job, often without a shred of guilt, while they're drawing a salary from the current company's payroll. They don't care that their actions will saddle their current employer with recruiting costs plus interviewing and training expenses. Some of these employees are so deceitful that if, or when, they get caught, they casually say they are preparing their curriculum vitae so that a friend who is actively looking for work can use it as a mock-up.

Messing up is human, and is not a sin, as far as I'm aware. But, being deceitful and disrespectful to your employer, your peers, and your co-workers leans more toward playing a game of high-stakes poker. And there are good reasons why we don't play poker on the job. Bluffing requires deceit, and if you think you can get away with lying, you may find out otherwise, to your own detriment.

Replaying these and other stories in my mind often brings about a mix of humour and disappointment. This is especially true when I think about Judy, the young lady who lost her job because she was upset with her co-worker for singing all the time. On more than one occasion Judy had asked the co-worker to stop singing because it was annoying her. Woefully, the vocalist did not share the same opinion of her own talents, and refused to oblige. One day, as the singing started again, Judy threatened to physically stitch her colleague's lips together if she didn't cease and desist. The moment her threat of physical harm was reported to management, Judy was summoned to the HR office. Her explanation for the physical threat was: "Oh no, the hummingbird didn't take what I said the way it was meant. It's all her fault for being a constant nuisance around here. Besides, she totally ignored my warning last week when I told her that if she didn't shut-up I'd slap her mouth." Wow!

Another incident that keeps surfacing in my mind is the story of a mobile officer who got caught using the company's gas card to fill up his own car. When confronted with proof of his furtive actions, his response was: "I don't see what the big deal is; the company has more money than I do." His logic held no shame, nor any responsibility to pay back the unauthorized spending.

Promises, promises

A fascinating variation on this theme has to do with field supervisors and middle management staff thoughtlessly promising their subordinates things they may not be able to deliver on. In their effort to promote progress and gain respect (or curry favour) from their team, they reel off promises of perks and improvements that are not in their power to grant. It's not uncommon to hear supervisors say to underlings that if they were in charge, they'd give them a pay raise. Supervisors should never promise what they're not authorized to deliver, because, in a best-case scenario, their failures will probably mar their relationship with the junior members. Worse yet, they could face reprimand and embarrassment from higher-ups or even lose their own job over it. Why make such statements when those employees didn't do anything exemplary to deserve a pay raise? What does a supervisor have to gain from remarking "If I was the boss," when they're not the boss? As far as I can tell, giving people false hope is not the way to build a strong company culture or help employees grow into better performers. Dexterity, facts, and know-how do that. Making empty promises may win a person of authority a few points in the short term, but it only disappoints people in the end. The way to create a strong company culture is to deal honestly with employees, manage expectations fairly, and do your best to set everyone up for success.

The danger of allowing supervisors to make empty promises without facing consequences is that they risk employee dissatisfaction and operational disruption. That kind of instability can endanger a company in the longer term. It happens time and time again that well-intentioned middle and senior managers drop the ball by allowing undeliverable promises to go unnoticed until their own reputation starts to take a hit. When we make a promise, we're making a commitment to do what we say we're going to do. People count on us to deliver on our promise, regardless of whether it takes us five, ten, or fifteen tries to get it done. When we fail to deliver on things as significant as a pay increase, it can have financial and emotional effects on people and create tangible setbacks.

There is nothing more important than integrity. A solid company reputation is a fundamental indicator of who we really are as people and as leaders. Besides, it's the company values that show how the brand promises to perform. It's no secret that some of us consider broken promises to be a politician's domain, but the truth is, this type of activity takes place pretty regularly in a lot of other areas and industries.

I clearly recall working for a distribution company many years ago, where a few members of the middle management team and two senior managers were legendary for overpromising and under-delivering. They weren't disciplined enough to follow through on their constant promises to approve vacation requests or to sign-off on guaranteed remuneration adjustments.

Furthermore, they did not make good on the redistribution of the lopsided workload, which caused ongoing frustration and conflicts among co-workers. Yet they were somehow perfectly able to keep their commitment to enjoy each other's company at a local bar every Friday. They did not just meet to knock back one, two, or three drinks and then run out the door; oh no!

They took their time to savour a Corpse Reviver #2 followed by a Sazerac, a Martini, and a Zombie. Life at this place of employment offered them good perks — or so it seemed. Before long, their weekly social engagements were noticeably affecting their performance, and eventually, their behaviour landed them in the foot soldier's office (the HR office). That was the end of their raucous fun-seeking. I bet, once they sobered up, they realized that on a good day, work missteps can be worrisome, but when you get yourself knee-deep in a doozie, you may have to turn to triple-strength Rolaids to relieve your emotional and financial indigestion.

It's true that every now and again, work can be a stressful place. It wouldn't be out of line to turn to comfort food, cigarettes, or a good stiff alcoholic beverage, in order to minimize the anxiety. But these are all solutions best practiced *outside* of work. Of course, there are times when these remedies will do the trick, but at other times, we lose the battle with nervous tension and allow stress to rob us of a decent night's sleep.

Of self-care and sick days

As we all know, a good night's sleep has just as much value as a good diet and exercise. Nowadays, because we have so much to do at work and at home, we tend to put sleep at the bottom of the list. In most cases, by the time we go to bed and complete our mental calculations of what we need to achieve the next day, the thought of getting enough sleep is not feasible any more. The bottom line here is, when we're short on sleep, we impair our body's ability to fend off sickness and we limit our capacity to think clearly. Those are the mornings when missed sleep makes it tough to get up and go.

Fortunately, some of us work at jobs that permit flexible start time or a generous number of sick days off. In that respect, it's a no brainer to head in late or even call in sick. Here, both the boss and HR will not question the real motive for being absent and the salary does not feel the pinch. In some instances, employers even recognize that certain occupations carry high stress levels, which can cause employee burnout; therefore, taking the odd fake sick-day off (sometimes called a mental health day) is justified. However, in most sectors, one may not be able to pull this off too often without a legitimate reason. A call-in to say you won't be at work because you forgot a doctor's appointment, or the baby-sitter didn't show up and you can't reach her, may not give you a free pass. Neither will the story that you didn't get any sleep the previous night and cannot function properly just yet, or that you have too much laundry to catch-up on and cannot leave the house. One excuse for skipping work that doesn't usually bode well (or go over well with employers or colleagues) is the one about feeling too upset to go to work because you just broke up with your boyfriend or girlfriend. Even though some employers will give their employees the benefit of the doubt about their call-in excuses, a good number of them will, in fact, put in the time and effort to check on the legitimacy of the 'sick' call. I've heard of instances where an employer received a call from an employee saying he was too sick to drive to work, and the employer's suspicion was so high that he actually got in the car and drove to the employee's house. Imagine the surprise when the employee's car had left the driveway and the knock on the door went unanswered. The following day, when the boss confronted the employee, he adamantly denied not being home. When asked a second and third time, he revised the answer and said that he had felt a short relief from the sickness and had driven to the nearby store to get juice. That day marked the end of their trusting relationship.

Other dubious excuses for taking a day off that are almost guaranteed to also cause a permanent rift between employer and employee include:

- Tried to dry my uniform in the oven and it caught fire
- Had a few drinks with friends last night and still feel dizzy
- Had trouble with a bowel movement this morning and had to sit on the toilet for a long time; that caused my feet to swell and go numb; now I cannot wear shoes
- Having abdominal pains and need time to heal them with homeopathic remedies; that process takes a long time
- Went gambling last night and lost all my money. I have no means to put fuel in the gas tank and come to work
- Cannot come to work because I want to take an emergency day off (in reality, this employee was simply making sure they used up one of their two days of paid personal emergency leave mandated by the Ontario government as of 2017; there was no emergency)
- I won't be at work today because my car doesn't start and I don't like taking the bus
- I cannot cover my shift because the weather is bad and my parents told me to stay home.

Every one of these excuses was actually offered to me or to an industry colleague.

According to an article published by Reuters Plus not long ago, approximately fifteen percent of employers in the United States have fired employees for frequent absenteeism owed to fake illness symptoms. Other surveys have also compared sick days in Canada and the United States, and found that Canadians take more. Most of the time, the absence is due to superficial reasons. As much as employers want to give their employees the benefit of the doubt, more than thirty percent have taken the time to check on the validity of the sick claim in some way or another. In other parts of the industrial world, twenty percent of employers have dismissed employees for continuously calling in sick with fake excuses. Then there are other employers who are more forgiving and prefer to only reprimand their employees for lying to them. Some employees get caught as a result of their online activities. Yet it's very difficult for an employer to gather proof in support of their suspicions with regards to fake illness absences. Without overwhelming proof, the malingering employee can be quite successful at evading disciplinary action. It is not rare to notice patterns of sick absences that last only a day so. For illnesses this short, the employee does not have to bring a doctor's note and doesn't draw too much attention to their poor attendance record. Yet the days add up and bite into the company's bottom line. These are some of the most common, one-day *"I'm sick"* excuses and situations that have caused me to shake my head over the years:

- An employee posts things on social media that do not match their being sick claim
- Employees calling in sick on Fridays or Mondays so they can have a long weekend
- A field supervisor being absent the day a new project begins. He clearly did not want to be responsible for detailing the requirements of the new project
- A technician takes a day off because he feels a migraine coming on and cannot drive. In reality, he does not want to address the pending complex system overhaul
- Employees who call in sick when any of the World Cup games are on
- Employees who didn't get their requested day off call in sick on that same day.

Ethics and values

Everyone's daily decision-making processes are tied into their own understanding of proper ethics and values. Ethics and values help nurture and develop our beliefs. Knowing and understanding our values makes it easier to choose what is right and what makes the most sense for us. For instance, if we value safety and security, there's a good chance we'll avoid going out alone for long walks at night. If we value our privacy, we'll refrain from giving out too much personal information, especially on social media. If we value good personal hygiene, we'll be sure to shower and wear clean clothes before going anywhere. If we value financial stability, we'll pass up risky behaviour like speculating and gambling.

In contrast, if we place importance on excitement, we're likely to take some risks. We'll be constantly on the lookout for new and exciting experiences, whether those involve work, family, or friends. If we value honesty, we will avoid lying, even if it will change the outcome of an unpleasant situation. For example, a parent obliterates the truth, lying to the authorities, in order to protect their child from having to do community work in lieu of payment for damaging school property. Although the parent may not be in the habit of lying, they allow themselves to make an exception for their child. It's an immature and ineffective way to address the problem, and it's one that can backfire spectacularly because it teaches the child that they can get away with misdeeds — that Mom or Dad will save them.

According to research and studies done by Joshua Greene, a Harvard cognitive neuroscientist, and Dan Airiely, a behavioural psychologist at Duke University, people turn to deception when the truth threatens to be troublesome. The problem is that, as their research has demonstrated, telling lies makes it easier to lie again. It's like feeding the blue whale; the more you feed it, the more it wants, and still, it always remains unfulfilled. Moreover, the truth about lying is that we are the real judges of our own honesty.

Dr. Bella DePaulo, Ph.D., a psychologist at the University of Virginia, argues that lying is as common and ordinary as brushing our teeth and that being one hundred percent honest is neither possible nor desirable. Believing that deceptive communications aren't always spoken with the intention to mislead, but are quite often guided by the same objective as truthful ones, Dr. DePaulo set out to explore the hypothesis that lying was part of everyday life and not a strange occurrence. To carry out her weeklong experiment, she sought 147paid participants.

The subject group was comprised of college students and community members ranging in age from eighteen to seventy-one. By the end of the week, the participants had recorded a combined total of 1,535 lies. The tally amounted to two lies a day for the college students and one lie a day for the community members. The study also concluded that people typically lie about their feelings, their actions, their immediate and long-term plans, and their whereabouts.

If we can extrapolate these numbers to the general population, this adds up to an exorbitant number of falsehoods floating around the world at any given time. Whereas, when honesty is used as the proper way of handling things, even if no one is watching us, I'd venture to say that the truth becomes the component central to building a solid personal relationship and the key element to make businesses prosper. Mark Twain wrote, "I have a higher and grander standard of principle than George Washington. He could not lie; I can, but I won't." Given how common research tells us lying is, it seems clear that people who live the way Twain claims to have lived are exceedingly, maybe even vanishingly, rare. It takes tremendous willpower and a firm grasp on one's own values and morals to tell the truth, even when the outcome may not favour you. It may be naïve or too tall an order to ask everyone to tell the truth all the time, especially when "little white lies" can save people's feelings, as I pointed out earlier in this book. But I believe that we should always strive to be honest, especially when our truth-telling won't hurt others, and we should know, also, that we may occasionally need to hurt our own interests or those of our loved ones in order to live according to the values of honesty. Think of the parent who lied for their child to cover for a vandalism charge. How much better would it have been for the child, in the long term, if the parent had allowed them to suffer a consequence for their actions? Honesty in matters of importance is a goal worth striving for, in business as in life.

CHAPTER 9

THE FACE OF DIFFERENT VALUES

Thanks are due to our parents, teachers and religious leaders for teaching us common values when we were children. They taught us how to love, how to play safely, to be creative, to have respect for people and property, the art of sharing and, most of all, the importance of telling the truth. However, some of those morals tend to get modified as we grow up and we begin to see the world in a different light.

Moral principles such as respect, love and friendship often undergo shifts as our demeanor changes and we figure out what is most important to us. At the same time as we manage our personal development, our standards tend to make progress toward our capacity to deal with missed opportunities and whatever else life has to offer. Upon reaching the young adult juncture, the need to advance toward life-changing modifications inspires us to choose personal core values that will take on a variety of principles and morality. Respect may take the form of tolerance; love can transform into gratitude; and friendship may become the listening ear that helps us filter-out things that waste time in our life. Although values are not known to be static, we can all remain authentic and effective individuals as long as our configuration of principles, thoughts, and behavior, are an expression of our best self.

Most endorsements of values, whether good or not so good, will change face over the years, with the exception of personal interaction. Collaboration, and the act of coming together in time of need, is an important adolescent value that doesn't seem to decrease very much with the passing of time.

As children, we learn about imagination, honesty, and standing up for ourselves and for those close to us. We're also sensitive to the needs of people who find themselves in a difficult situation through no fault of their own. Dillon, my twelve-year-old grandson, affirmed the meaning of standing up for those who unexpectedly find themselves in a precarious situation when he was seven years old. While playing with his friends in the schoolyard one day, he noticed one of his classmates being bullied by a slightly older boy. Without hesitation or the slightest concern for his own safety, he jumped to the little girl's defense. Dillon got between them and pushed the boy away, urging him to stop picking on his friend. He stood ready to defend himself in the event the boy chose to challenge him. His quick and selfless reaction to that unfair scene meant so much to the young girl that the sight of someone being there and looking out for her made her feel like she could breathe again. Her huge sighs of relief could be heard from a distance. Dillon's instinctive act told her it wasn't her fault for being picked on, and most importantly, she was reassured that she wasn't so alone, and that if someone bullied her, he would be there to help. It goes without saying that the older boy's unhealthy habit of treading on someone's toes as a way of making his presence known did not serve him well that day. The bully learned a valuable lesson about the consequences that may arise from snarled values, and he never picked on that little girl again.

There's an old proverb that says: "If you want happiness for an hour, take a nap. If you want happiness for a day, go fishing. If you want happiness for a year, inherit a fortune. If you want happiness for a lifetime, help somebody." Those who stand willing to help others often do so because they were taught to believe in the values of kindness, fair-dealing, equity, and charity.

Although values come in different forms, they really are the foundation of all conduct. They tell us how to live and work and they inform our social ideals. Without a set of values and principles that we hold dear enough to defend, our daily lives wouldn't be worth much. Furthermore, values that are claimed but left unused are just as worthless as not having any at all. Beliefs and principles have a knack for seeping into the examination of decency to such extent that most of us automatically assume a person with values is a good person. On the whole, that theory holds true. We admire people who live according to their values, even when the situation may work out to their loss.

I know of a not-so-well-off young lady who, when leaving a superstore one day, noticed a twenty-dollar bill on the floor by the exit door. Because she believed in honesty, she picked up the money and brought it to the cashier. She explained where she had found it and asked the cashier to hold on to it in the event the person who had lost it retraced their steps and came back to claim it. In my view, that's an act of uprightness! Not only did she not take what wasn't hers, but she tried to find the bill's owner, even though she could have used the money herself.

In contrast, sometimes breaking away from our pre-set values is not necessarily a bad thing. There are instances when the end result is what highlights the terms of our morality. What this means is that it may be good to break a principle or do without sincerity in situations where our actions will produce wholesome results. Let's look at a scenario: Whether by accident or on purpose, you've been privy to information that will cause damage to your employer, or a family member, or a friend. Does breaking the 'no tattletale' rule protect the unsuspecting people from unnecessary suffering? I vote yes! But, for the ill-intended person, this may be a disappointment and a breakdown of their sneaky moral code. Nonetheless, contrary to their devious standards, I would consider this act of moral sponsorship a desirable quality. Let's face it; does short-circuiting a tight-lipped promise that carries the potential of harm really qualify as an untrustworthy act? I say not! I don't even believe that it's as offensive as calling in sick to work and putting on a fake cough or a slurred speech claiming to be running a fever. It's even less offensive than putting on a deep nasal voice to feign congestion so as to justify taking a fake sick-day off work. Obviously, virtue and ethics put us on the hook to tell the truth and to keep our promises all the time, but there has to be some allowance made for situations when there's no better choice available than to forfeit the promise.

Whether we realize it or not, words and information have power. When used in the proper context and for the right reason, and *only* the right reason, everyone will benefit from the outcome. When we misuse their influence, we risk eroding our trust and it could turn out to be a big deal for all parties involved. I'd say that it's in everyone's best interest to take a brief moment and think before saying things out loud, if only to avoid leaving burned bridges along the way.

Ethics, behaviour, and opinions are apt to change over time, and within a given situation. The question then becomes: who's to decide what should change and what constitutes a justifiable reason for change? Whose duty will it be to level those changes with the general public, since they most certainly will touch upon religious views, business operations, the role of medical and legal professionals, policing, parenthood, information technology, educational theories, and the way we care for the elderly and the disadvantaged?

For example: a business with misaligned financial practices boasts about their stable and successful operational framework. In reality, that's hardly the case, but the owner's ego is spared. On a parallel line, we'll find that personal explanations run along the same vantage points. Have you ever had to explain to a friend the reason you didn't answer the text about buying hockey tickets? The purposely distorted truth about your phone failing you will inevitably be overshadowed by the fact you didn't want him to know your finances are a mess and you're broke. How many times have we blurted out "how nice to see you again" to someone we could care less about?

The truth is, we say it because we want to be cordial and want them to feel like they matter to us. Another instance where the truth tends to get stretched quite a bit is when someone asks a friend how many people they've slept with. There is no doubt the number given is either inflated or grossly understated depending on who's asking and who's answering.

So, does a broadened image of the truth make the response a bad thing? Not necessarily. I think it's a matter of personal preference. However, answering your partner's question about a purchase with vagueness like, "the item was on sale and didn't cost very much," is more of a grayish lie because you purposely attempt to circumvent the question about how much you paid for that eye-catching necklace you didn't need. And what do we make of the pristine little lies parents tell children when they won't eat their vegetables? Does telling the children that vegetables are actually adult dessert and if they eat it; they'll get big like Mommy and Daddy, represent a different face of our prized values? Let's not leave out the fibs we tell children when we don't want to replace the drained battery of a noisy toy; we tell them that the store is all out of those batteries and that they will call us when the new ones arrive. Then, we craftily put the toy away and hope that out-of-sight will mean out-of-mind for a long time. These slight distortions of the truth are told as an acceptable explanation given to ease our own feelings of guilt and to support the notion that our actions were necessary in order to achieve the greater good.

So, if my understanding of what really matters in our personal life and at the place of work is correct, then I think it's safe to say that breaking a basic rule or a promise to keep a secret is not, in itself, the worst thing we can do. Even if values take on a different face at one special time or another in our life, we always have the option to re-direct our focus on the method which best guides our actions forward to achieve the best results.

Over and above sorting through the dissimilarities we come across at different stages in our life, I would say that we're also faced with making modifications to the strength of our principles as we reach a mature adult age. Although taking these extra steps may not feel like the most desirable way to go through the ageing process, nevertheless, it's representative of life's real progression. I'm experiencing first-hand just how values sometimes need to be re-apportioned, and in some cases replaced with more appropriate ones, to make room for current needs.

Making adjustments to better reflect the requirements of our age is very much like renegotiating the terms of a marriage in order to promote a long-lasting union. As an example, change may lead retired adults to be grateful for traditions as a way of adding new meaning to their life while they try to distance themselves from the responsibilities they managed in their younger years. Obligations such as raising a family, working hard to advance the career, making good on mortgage payments and planning for a solid education for the children are now someone else's footprints. Those tasks have now become voiceless points that get in the way of moving forward to accurately reflect the present needs and physical abilities. In the same vein, we find that the crisp ideas and hurried activities that energized us in our younger years are asking to be excused. We can allocate more time to take care of our well-being and learn to be mindful of our safety, dietary requirements, and include a little quiet time for short naps during the days.

The real question here is: How does one figure out which is the best way to deal with this significant change? We may search and probably find many answers to this question, but how will we know which one is right for us? Is there a special seminar available that teaches us how to remain engaged in life and not slant toward the brass tacks of what we can no longer do?

Although we may want to put up a fight and not accept with grace that getting older calls on our five senses to seek out adjustments and re-alignment, we should be thankful for the medical advances that have made it possible to successfully treat most of our physical ailments, with the exception of weight gain, hair loss, and overall loss of energy.

Words and deeds change as we get older. Once we join the ranks of "the elderly," we voluntarily set aside the old desire for sweet words and have less need to be the centre of attention. Those of us who endorse a makeover in our values not only give meaning to the more mature lifestyle, but are ready to concede that one phase of our life is ending and that we're ready for the next phase.

This maturation process can open up a space for new core values. We adopt more formal procedures by believing we've reached a contented stage in our life and we don't necessarily need to retain so much of the so-called spunk any longer. We follow that trend by getting through the long days with the comfort of our peer's company and playing board games. By this time, what we once knew as romance has become companionship. Moreover, our bodies start to talk back, and we begin to complain about our feet being cold and about how our toes keep cramping. We have long lists of laments. Our Maalox didn't work very well that day, or the sciatic nerve is acting up, or arthritis is trying to take ownership of our joints. At this point, the thrill of spending time with the person who could make things better for us revolves around a peaceful night at home and an early bedtime of between nine-thirty and ten post meridiem.

In the mornings, habitual conversation starters in our age group twirl around nature's knock-on effects, such as a decline in muscle mass, manifestation of wrinkles, hearing loss, diminished eyesight, memory loss, sleeplessness nights, frequent trips to the bathroom, and gastric problems, to mention only some of the highlights. Now, the trick for success is not as much a mystery as it is common sense. For all intents and purposes, by taking a reasonable approach at reinventing ourselves and learning to adapt to new routines, we can put a positive spin on these and other changes, keep our sense of humour, and continue to enjoy life just fine, thank you very much.

Let's take a brief minute to look at how values can shift for seniors who manage to make their seventies and eighties the new sixties. They give us a lot to think about as we watch them redefine aging. I find it almost impossible to ignore the fact that a good number of today's senior citizens are a product of the baby boomer generation. In my opinion, they are the men and women whose earlier days were driven by hard work, a desire for betterment, and a wish for independence. They were in control of their own lives, believed in fair play, and worked hard toward economic growth. Today, as their mobility begins to slip away from them, they're faced with the expectation to make every possible effort to progress toward digital literacy and fit into the virtual environment by learning how to connect with their children and grandchildren via Zoom, text, and all other manner of tech and platforms. These one-time defenders of the social order now find themselves in the position of beginners again, learning what amounts to a foreign language. Some are in sync with the concept and grasp that the use of online communication with their family does not come easily, nor is it mastered with one or two tries. Without a lot of practice, this new know-how can prove elusive. For the most part, the fear of getting things wrong or messing up the electronic tools can cause the elderly to suffer paralyzing fear of digitization. The majority will take a back seat to this method of revolutionary contact, while the more determined ones will rise to the challenge. Unlike the members of today's digital society, in their younger days, the only technological thing most baby boomers managed was probably the channel and volume buttons of a television set. It's natural that even the prospect of learning basic internet browsing skills fills them with nostalgia for simpler times.

When interacting with seniors, whether in the capacity of a caregiver or a guardian, I believe we can do well to avoid conversations relating to computer jargon, along the lines of 'cloud storage,' 'electronic harmonization' and a whole lot of other technical concepts. Instead, we can engage seniors in dialogue about their past hobbies, ask them about old friends, or get them talking about memories of their working life, if they were career-oriented in their younger years. If the elderly person enjoyed music in their yesteryears, we could play one or more of their favourite melodies, and I bet we'll see them tap their feet and clap their hands.

Although that tune represents a part of the past they can never go back to, it's not so strange to see them raise their shoulders up and down or paste a smile on their face. Yes, music has the power to evoke strong emotions and it will often bring back happy memories. If photography was their number one pastime, we can show them photo albums full of snapshots from their past and we'll see their eyes peel back so far that we'll get the impression we just opened a window to their soul.

Those simple gestures symbolize the most up-to-date significance of their newly redefined values. Material things that once played a key role in their lives, such as a home on a large lot with full grown trees, a reliable and classy car, a successful career, or a fully stocked wine cellar, now have taken a tumble and landed squarely at the bottom of their wish list. The thing that remains unwavering at the top of their life's directory is love for their family, watching the news, and the desire for tranquility, a financial safety net, and of course, physical comfort as well as mental and emotional reassurance.

I've lost count of the number of times I've heard people say that age is just a number. In general, that's true, but after we celebrate a certain birthday, practical considerations weigh in, and we seem to adopt new habits and peculiarities— most of which we thought only applied to other older people. Not us! We're not agents of change yet! There must be other justifiable reasons for not keeping our balance when putting on our pants, moving dinner time to 5:00p.m., and for leaving long-winded messages on the children's voicemail. The same rationalization applies for wearing a sweater and thermal socks when the temperature dips to twenty-two degrees Celsius, and for drinking a lot of water during the day and then making frequent trips to the bathroom during the night.

The moral of the story is that values develop different features as time passes. An activity that was once labeled a 'blast' today serves as a reminder of the time that has passed. There are many reasons why people should not grow impatient with seniors; they're trying to figure things out; that's why they're not fond of waiting in line at the grocery store and don't appreciate being honked at because they drive 40 miles per hour in a 60-mph zone. Sometimes, it's the way we talk to seniors — or talk about them — that makes them feel like they're being sidelined or marginalized. Treating the elderly with respect and speaking to them in normal tones will create a respectful relationship. This means avoiding "elder-talk" (baby talk for seniors), calling them pet names like ducky or whippersnapper, referring to them by any number of anti-senior slurs (geezer, oldster), or speaking slowly and stretching out each syllable. Let's give them the courtesy of listening to what they have to say, treat them like the experienced adults that they are, and steer clear of making judgements. We must keep in mind that today's elderly were yesterday's driving force who dared to spread hope, plucked up the courage to dream big, and lived out their ambitions.

Having the openness to embrace old age is what lays the groundwork for a healthy and meaningful quality of life. This presence of mind can, and will, affect not only our personal behavior as we move along in our days, but will make evident the need for remodeling our business principles as well.

A seasoned entrepreneur will put forth a formidable range of experience and wisdom to ensure that the end results outweigh the obligations. The mere fact that these operators have survived many stints in the foxholes over the years makes their experience a priceless resource. Many a hardened industrialist has been able to succeed without the advantage of electronic communication. Their network wizardry says that nothing beats a personal meeting to either open or close a business deal. They've seen it, they've done it, and they've heard of it. They played a tough game when no one else wanted to play, and they won skirmishes that threatened their stability. The good news is that their abilities do not remain frozen in time; most of them would be ready and willing to cross into the digitalized space with a little help from a mentor. Whether the operation is a large corporation or a small entity, if we choose to ignore the value of change, we expose ourselves to the risk of missing the opportunity in which to strengthen the reliability of the environment.

Having trekked through my business journey for the last thirty plus years, I readily own up to the fact that change of practices and work protocols have brought a lot of validation to the industrial world and to the business owners as well as the CEOs and top management teams of any organization. One thing that stands out to me is the nerve some people display as they uncharitably theorize about what public values for corporate and political entities should look like. I'm referring to the individuals who believe their place of employment should pay employees top dollar regardless of their participation, the type of industry, or their bottom line. Let's also look at what some people will endorse where government spending is concerned. I've come across many individuals who endorse enhanced spending for one sector but not another. For example: they lend support for extra spending for the education system but not agriculture or climate change.

Then, they quickly switch to neutral mode and entertain dissimilar practices for their own personal conduct. These are the same individuals who will sing a different tune when their own personal conduct comes under scrutiny. They find fault with other people's policies but rarely hold themselves to the same standards. Take for instance, people who go to work just because they have to. They have no regard for loyalty and no desire to contribute to the company's bottom line, or to adhere to the company protocols and guidelines. However, they keenly foster the "me first" ideology and are ready to sue the employer the minute someone mistakenly utters a word they find offensive.

The endgame here is that this dual set of standards may cause confusion for some, whereas others find it quite acceptable to send out a twofold guidebook of acceptable practices without any ambition to shoot beyond their mixed messages. They have one set of rules for their own personal benefit and another set for select institutions and business organizations. But, if the objective is to get personal gains from a given plan, well, then, is it not reasonable to assume that endorsing a dual-part system might be a way of getting personal gains at the expense of others? That can't bode too well for values or righteousness!

To theorize about practicing appropriate corporate values is not the same as saying that an individual is one hundred percent knowledgeable about how to apply the correct business practices or how to measure accuracy when addressing transactions with imposters of business fitness. The concept is made even harder because one never knows if the most sensible outcome will prevail, or if the long thought-out plan will get tossed out like a dirty rag by those who oppose every word said and every suggestion made. Even when the proceedings are met with a one-two punch, there could be enough griping to go around when the ones seeking to apply the most refined operational standards discover they're on a collision course with those who cannot, and will not, comprehend the advantages of reaching common ground. Sad to say, any consideration to call-out those individuals on the disrespect of the moment and their disregard for the issue at hand does not guarantee a positive outcome. I know this because I've taken more than one turbulent ride on the rollercoaster we call business.

In a split second, I could list-off many reasons why, over the years, I've come to look at various operation modifications as a redundant waste of time. I can tell you for certain that not only did some sugar-coated, fine-tuned effort not help me get a clear-cut answer to a half-loaded business question, but any hope of making sense of those talking points with a disinterested party definitely failed. How does one get the message across that choosing to attack an employer's priorities and work models only succeeds in causing disorder and distractions, while slowing down everyone involved?

Many moons ago, when I first stepped on the business escalator, it was much simpler to learn the commerce rules and labour regulations in place at the time. The list of dos and don'ts was a lot shorter than the never-ending one we have to contend with today. Under-performers were not allowed to fester on the team too long, especially when it was believed that the situation would not correct itself. Today, the proper way to address the issue is to softly approach the individual with a speech along the lines of, "I'm noticing some issues with your work, is there anything I can do to help?" or "I've noticed your performance is slipping a bit and maybe it's partly my fault for not mentioning it sooner. What can we do to get out of this tailspin?" The answer may well be: "I'm doing the best I can and this is who I am." The employer is now left with the decision of whether to keep them or dismiss them, and at what cost? There's also a slim chance that the employee will take a few days to digest the substance and the value of the conversation and report back to the boss with some suggestions for improvement. On a good day, this shows the employee has genuine interest in keeping their job and working to turn things around. Now it's up to the manager to do regular follow-ups on the promised progress and keep the details of the arrangement confidential.

In the old days, an employer had supplemental leeway to push back where excuses for deficiency were on hand, and they had the margin to say that their directive was not up for debate. Furthermore, a call-in to the boss's office did not mean it was a boss-versus-employee scenario; it was mostly about the boss having a say. With that protocol in place, service providers and their employees clearly understood the employment protection standards available to them, and legal battles were few and far between. Neither side needed to consult a legal expert to decipher the intricacies of the rules so each could find an angle in which to undermine the other. All summed up, the criteria to move the company forward in a disciplined and successful manner spoke the language of people who believe in continuous progress.

Besides all that, in the security industry, one of the measures best known to push the agenda forward was the desire to assemble a team comprised of sales representatives, field staff, and administrative personnel capable of making society feel safe. Today, a lot has changed, but one thing has stayed the same: the necessity and the value of providing a secure environment for company owners, their family, their employees, and anyone who is aware of their security requirements and is ready to take action to make good on the need. It's with thanks to the proactive individuals who follow through with their plans to prioritize the security and safety of people and premises that society can breathe a sigh of relief. These individuals don't hem and haw about making a decision in the name of safety and then get all financially keyed-up and put it on hold to approve a less important project —one that might make them a little more noticeable as 'the' person with sovereignty. If and when they're called upon to explain their decision, they'll quickly point the finger at "choice fatigue." The decision-makers who regard security as a priority give the stamp of approval for the expenditures that creates a positive setting for the overall well-being of the people they work with and of those they lead. At the end of the day, it's hard to dispute the fact that security provides peace of mind and the decisions we make regarding this prerequisite determines our reality in life. Electronic security systems have been an exigency for a long time now, and the demand continues to grow as the need to beef up threat detection and damage prevention is being taken ever so seriously by the social order. As sophisticated technology becomes a hot item, so too must the need to overhaul the old government training programs step up to that reality. Rebranding the industry to better deal with the new safety and security requirements cannot be accomplished through the use of outdated models. A serious facelift is needed to meet the challenges of the job.

To maintain a solid performance profile, the security sector has been calling for discussions regarding the new norm and to figure out the extra steps to be taken in order to minimize the risks and the vulnerability that might befall the company or its employees. It's not in anyone's best interest to simply lower the service bar because it's too cumbersome to question outdated security principles and labour guidelines that have remained un-debated and untouched by The Ministry of Community Safety and Correctional Services officials for far too long.

As much as I give credence to the idea that service contributors should not be made to feel trapped and unable to perform to their maximum capacity due to stale regulation roadblocks, I've come to the conclusion that the best approach is to put enough safeguards in place to create the safest and best working environment possible while we keep waiting for renewed regulations that better suit the industrial and commercial sectors. The idea is to apply whichever business procedures and ethics go hand-in-hand with the stale directives because the new ones can't seem to get off the ground and boogie around everything else that doesn't fit the mold. Because it's not advisable to target or disregard the existing labour structure of the business sector, business owners and upper management must remain vigilant and not reinforce the very problems we're trying to eliminate. The fact of the matter is that modernizing labour standards can be a slow process that requires multiple negotiating efforts and at times even calls on the expertise of legal counsel.

As Bruce Lee once said, "A fight is not won by one punch or kick. Either learn to endure or hire a bodyguard."

It makes total sense that progressive transitioning toward a winning strategy may take a certain amount of investment both in time and money. This often means that to reach our objective it may take more than one or two tries to facilitate the preferred outcome. But, when multiple tries don't produce the anticipated results, then seeking help from the tried and true experts will put us in a better position to realize the desired results.

Another thing not to be overlooked is the fact that in the present day, managing a service company and trying to stay a step ahead of an underhanded situation is much more complicated and demanding than it was years ago. From an operational standpoint, if I were to not accept 'no' for an answer to a request for a change of course, or continue applying yesterday's rules of functionality in today's market, I'd definitely be looking for a permanent migraine. Instead, as much as I consider some current operative rebranding unfair, I look at modifications as something that inspires me to do what needs to be done in a bid to thrive in this new landscape.

It's a fragile art to try to compare yesterday's less sophisticated methods of business operation to today's fast-moving digital environment. With marketing technologies popping up at a rapid pace, according to a survey by Constant Contact, Inc., an online marketing firm based in the United States, fifty-five to sixty percent of small businesses don't necessarily have an easy time adopting the new technology. The same number reported feeling uncomfortable putting their ideas on autopilot in order to reach an audience far beyond their familiarity.

Years ago, scaling a business was by no means easy to do. There were mornings when I woke up and wished that yesterday's problem— which was still waiting for me the next day, had moved on to become someone else's pickle. Because I didn't think it wise to admit any uneasiness, I put on a determined face and took charge of the situation. Before I could afford to bring in a human resources centre, I spoke directly to the staff or issued the necessary memos to update them on upcoming changes, such as policy modifications and new procedures. I did this all without over-thinking its presentation. Today, the communication technique must have an official look, has to portray a very concise message, and needs to mirror all the concerns of the intended audience. It should also be free of anything that might resemble finger-pointing, and most of all, it should pass the scrutiny of the vice president of the people (HR). What's more, in the present day, having a candid conversation with an employee regarding their performance issues or the need to improve personal hygiene is a real challenge for many business leaders. At times, it's much easier to sweep the problem under the rug than it is to attempt to work out the conflict. Before any boss-to-employee conversations takes place, management must ensure they have chosen all the correct words, filtered-out any possibly offensive verbiage, and selected only the use of politically correct and approved body language. What a journey a two- minute conversation can turn out to be!

The industry has changed in other ways, too. The areas that once occupied uncertain space between what people could do and could not do, industries that were designated for men only, house chores that were labeled women's territory, professional and political titles that were for men only, are not so sheltered or hidebound anymore. Today, everyone can grow in the field of their choice if only they're prepared to work hard and not give up on their objective when things get messy.

Now, when I engage in business conversations with my son and my daughter, whether the subject has to do with the run-of-the-mill financial matters, operational concerns, or a simple venting session, I can't help but think back at the daring attitude I must have had many years ago. Without product knowledge or financial backing, I asserted my position in a field totally foreign to female operators: the security industry. Although there is a longstanding mantra that says you should have industry know-how before you venture into your own business, not everyone follows that theory. I know I didn't. I was an outsider in the security racket, with no preconceived notions and no field expertise. But, I was determined and willing to learn a great deal about strategies and industry insight so I could transform my initiative into a worthwhile business. I recall opening the door to my office on that first day of operation with nothing more than a novice viewpoint of how I would take on this new and unfamiliar field and how I could best go about setting up my own course. I knew I had to unblock my path and develop a way forward without getting in my own way. So, with an appetite for maneuvering, I became immersed in the foreground work and managed to bring every task to completion— some with success and some not so much. I carried out my tasks without ever uttering comments such as "this is not part of my job" or "I don't know how to do this."

I am a fan of Clay Clark's work in his book, *The Wheel of Wealth*. This is what he had to say about starting your own business: "Starting a successful business is not tricky. Starting a successful business does not require above average intellect. Starting a successful business does require having a pig-headed, purpose-driven tenacity about achieving your life goals and fulfilling your life's vision through providing products and services that offer uncompromising quality in a scalable and duplicatable way." In short, he told us to make sure one has the right combination and is a doer. Intent, by itself, does not help us take the next step and definitely does not meet the criteria to enter into the business arena. In that field, failures and setbacks are the biggest motivators — not what pushes us to give up.

Putting all that aside, the reality is that after many years in this business, I've gained a new set of perspectives on things. A lot has changed for the better. Today, anyone can make rank, and no one need be invisible. Although disharmony can reach weird proportions at times, for the most part, all that's required to aid us in being able to achieve our goal is the desire to bring an idea to life, take ownership of high-minded standards, practice solid values, and have the drive to grasp the dynamics of what makes us tick.

People who want to, can elect to live in a world that is short on reality. However, let's not discount the fact that an enterprising entity has a way of making people wakeup to a different actuality and adhere to a unique set of values. In the business circle, what we envision to be an easy development or a quick dollar gain for personal satisfaction can suddenly become a vision wrongly imagined. In its place, what we become alerted to is this: the confirmation that the road to entrepreneurship can be insensitive and far-reaching at times. It can be relentlessly demanding, and frequently leaves us disillusioned. Owning and managing your own company is not only a financial concern. It's also an emotional investment.

For many proprietors as well as persons in the upper management circle, their work represents their life, and any failures or unmet expectations become a personal affront. Bouts of disappointment are not uncommon, and when they come around, the leader puts on a forced happy face and quickly conjures up positive solutions for the sake of the team. And *that* is the real business blueprint. Still, I can't think of a better way to build endurance and learn how not to let your emotions jump ahead of the facts.

When I first began writing this book I felt a little ill-at-ease talking about my daily face-to-face encounters with challenging business occurrences as well as employees' comments that more often than not only create controversy and disappointments. I spent a great deal of time weighing the pros and cons that my stories would carry the strength and ability to impact others and, if any of it could be a game changer for anyone. I repeatedly asked myself whether, in spirit, people would be interested to read about how I saw the business sector bring on change and how the industrial sphere is performing after the change. Admittedly, there were times during the writing process when I considered dropping this laborious task. Once my head cleared, I realized that this commitment was my way of opening a discussion about essential business operational dos and don'ts, talk about the necessity to develop the skill in which to make quality decisions with limited truthful information, and the means to transfer acquired knowledge. This project also offered an opportunity to share my experiences with those who may be involved in similar situations, and for those who may perhaps want to learn from them so that in the future, they can decode these lessons and turn them into useful procedures.

Experience, when backed by the ability to adapt to change, makes the best tutor we can have both in our careers and our personal life.

Peter Michael Senge, an American systems scientist and founder of the Society for Organizational Learning, commented that "collaboration is vital to sustain what we call profound or really deep change, because without it, organizations are just overwhelmed by the forces of the status quo."

A rather audacious realization hit me one morning while I was writing a chapter in this book. I realized that conditions that felt so foreign and difficult in the first decades of running my own business still remain very familiar to this day. In a perfect world, business should be an easy way to make money, should have low risks, and everyone should be able to choose between the right way and the wrong way to approach things. But, the reality is that whatever selection one makes can be subjective. Even worse, how does one properly and correctly examine the unending daily issues and proficiently figure out what to do without breaking a sweat? The indicator I used years ago, which told me it was time to put that issue on hold and move on to something else, is the same gauge I use today; if my head starts to feel heavy and my stomach burns, I know I need to switch files. By keeping such awareness alive, I manage to fuel my enthusiasm, appreciate the better parts of my life and my career, and champion the idea that off-putting occurrences don't last forever and neither do the positive ones.

Days come and days go. Time passes us by without asking for permission, and nothing stays the same forever. It's so important to remind ourselves that confronting harsh possibilities doesn't always have to be a dispiriting experience, because nothing is everlasting. We cannot deny nor ignore the fact that sooner or later we're all prone to face difficulties brought on through no fault of our own, and a quick fix may be out of our control.

Although we are men and women of proneness and routine, there will be times in our life when we're hard-pressed to find the energy to leap out of what holds us back. By taking small steps and turning them into revolutionary changes, we may bring forth aching trials and plenty of worry, but these challenges can help us keep our values alive.

ACKNOWLEDGEMENTS

To write about past and present personal experiences can be both a joyful and a difficult undertaking. It is a reminder of days gone by, a testament to our ability to remove life's hurdles, and a story of the personal sacrifices levied on oneself, one's family, and one's close friends.

I could not have written this book without the vital encouragement from many special people.

I'm thankful for the patience and support my husband, Enzo, showcased throughout this project. I'm sure he's relieved to know it's finally done!

To my children, Sabina and David, you make an outstanding support team. Thank you for making me realize that what I have written are not just words and sentences used to fill blank pages.

Thank you to Pierre Claude from Les Éditions Paulines, for being a one-person spirit squad, and for sharing your valuable thoughts and subject expertise with me.

Many thanks go to David and Susan Aiken, who on more than one occasion have made my writing a much more enjoyable experience.

A big thank you to all the people who stood with me through this journey and who, from the bottom of their heart, shared in my passion for writing and reading books.